D0861838

To David and Robin with Kris and Kayla,
to Beverly and Jonathan and Elizabeth
and to Holly and Michael.
May you, my children and your families,
continue to grow in the knowledge of
"this love that surpasses knowledge"
(Ephesians 3:19)

EPHESIANS

THE IVP NEW TESTAMENT COMMENTARY SERIES

WALTER L. LIEFELD

GRANT R. OSBORNE, SERIES EDITOR

D. STUART BRISCOE AND HADDON ROBINSON,
CONSULTING EDITORS

IVP Academic

An imprint of InterVarsity Press
Downers Grove, Illinois

InterVarsity Press
P.O. Box 1400, Downers Grove, IL 60515-1426
World Wide Web: www.ivpress.com
E-mail: email@ivpress.com

©1997 by Walter L. Liefeld

InterVarsity Press® is the book-publishing division of InterVarsity Christian Fellowship/USA®, a movement
of students and faculty active on campus at hundreds of universities, colleges and schools of nursing in the
United States of America, and a member movement of the International Fellowship of Evangelical Students.
For information about local and regional activities, write Public Relations Dept., InterVarsity Christian
Fellowship/USA, 6400 Schroeder Rd., P.O. Box 7895, Madison, WI 53707-7895, or visit the IVCF
website at <www.intervarsity.org>.

Design: Cindy Kiple
Images: Einzug in Jerusalem—Entry into Jerusalem by Wilhelm Morgner at Museum am Ostwall,
    Dortmund, Germany. Erich Lessing/Art Resource, NY.

ISBN 978-0-8308-4010-6

Printed in the United States of America ∞

Library of Congress Cataloging-in-Publication Data

Liefeld, Walter L.
  Ephesians/Walter L. Liefeld.
    p. cm.—(The IVP New Testament commentary series)
  Includes bibliographical references.
  ISBN 0-8308-1810-3 (cloth: alk. paper)
  1. Bible. N.T. Ephesians—Commentaries. I. Title. II. Series.
  BS2695.3.L54   1996
  227'.507—dc20

                                                              96-16869
                                                                   CIP

| P | 18 | 17 | 16 | 15 | 14 | 13 | 12 | 11 | 10 | 9 | 8 | 7 | 6 | 5 | 4 | 3 | 2 | 1 |
| Y | 25 | 24 | 23 | 22 | 21 | 20 | 19 | 18 | 17 | 16 | 15 | 14 | 13 | 12 | 11 | 10 |

General Preface

In an age of proliferating commentary series, one might easily ask why add yet another to the seeming glut. The simplest answer is that no other series has yet achieved what we had in mind—a series to and from the church, that seeks to move from the text to its contemporary relevance and application.

No other series offers the unique combination of solid, biblical exposition and helpful explanatory notes in the same user-friendly format. No other series has tapped the unique blend of scholars and pastors who share both a passion for faithful exegesis and a deep concern for the church. Based on the New International Version of the Bible, one of the most widely used modern translations, the IVP New Testament Commentary Series builds on the NIV's reputation for clarity and accuracy. Individual commentators indicate clearly whenever they depart from the standard translation as required by their understanding of the original Greek text.

The series contributors represent a wide range of theological traditions, united by a common commitment to the authority of Scripture for Christian faith and practice. Their efforts here are directed toward applying the unchanging message of the New Testament to the ever-changing world in which we live.

Readers will find in each volume not only traditional discussions of authorship and backgrounds, but useful summaries of principal themes and approaches to contemporary application. To bridge the gap between commentaries that stress the flow of an author's argument but skip over exegetical nettles and those that simply jump from one difficulty to another, we have developed our unique format that expounds the text in uninterrupted form on the upper portion of each page while dealing with other issues underneath in verse-keyed notes. To avoid clutter we have also adopted a social studies note system that keys references to the bibliography.

We offer the series in hope that pastors, students, Bible teachers and small group leaders of all sorts will find it a valuable aid—one that stretches the mind and moves the heart to ever-growing faithfulness and obedience to our Lord Jesus Christ.

Author's Preface

It suddenly struck me as I prepared to write this preface that the general editor and two of the authors of this series were once my students. It has now been my privilege to learn from them. This is a reminder that part of our calling in Christ is to minister to one another so that the whole body of Christ may "grow up into him who is the Head." Although imperfectly, I have tried to be part of this ongoing process of edification as both a teacher and a pastor. The goal of this commentary series has helped to draw together in my thinking not only these two worlds of seminary and church but also the worlds of Christianity and the non-Christian "universe next door." My study of Ephesians, already one of the inner circle of my "favorite" New Testament books, has been immeasurably (to use a Pauline superlative) enriching. I hope that you, the reader, will be stimulated to probe more deeply than my time, space and ability have permitted and to think of illustrations and applications far beyond the reach of my limited experience and imagination.

In the early 1950s it was my privilege to serve as a staff member with the young, vibrant and growing InterVarsity Christian Fellowship. As a lone itinerant I tried to reach students for Christ and foster the growth of Christians in four states in the Midwest and then in New York and

New Jersey. It is a singular joy to have InterVarsity Press now publish a written contribution of mine. I wish to express gratitude to every leader in the Fellowship, past and present, and also to my former colleagues and students. James Hoover of IVP receives my great appreciation and thanks for his patience and wisdom.

The most recent church I served was Christ Church in Lake Forest, Illinois. They shared me first with Trinity Evangelical Divinity School, during the last years of my several decades there, and then with this book. To general editor Grant Osborne, esteemed colleague at Trinity and cherished friend, and to consulting editor Stuart Briscoe, delightful friend and perceptive manuscript reader, I offer my gratitude.

The lofty, soaring themes of Ephesians can be sighted but never completely captured by any human author. I have tried to write in a way that will help the reader keep these themes in mind even when focusing on details. Once when the remarkable New Testament scholar F. F. Bruce was visiting for a time at our home, then in Long Island, he agreed to speak at our midweek church meeting. Because I was giving a series on Colossians, he offered to speak on that epistle. In the space of less than an hour he gave an exposition of the whole book! Colossians was never the same for us. And Ephesians, likewise, must be seen as a whole. The church, its ministries, God's grace, our conversion, our growth, the spiritual warfare—everything covered in that wonderful book must be seen from the perspective of the "heavenly realms." May this commentary carry us up, beyond itself, to those realms where Christ is exalted.

Introduction

More than any other book in the Bible, Ephesians displays the great purpose and plan of God for the church. It provides a perspective that is unique: God's—and the believer's—view from the "heavenly realms." This perspective may be thought of as the vertical dimension, and the plan of God as the linear dimension, of the book. This plan and perspective are more significant for determining the main subject or theme of Ephesians than are the various topics usually proposed. It is true, for example, that the book contains important teaching about the church and about Christian maturity, and it is possible to outline the book around such themes. But the major distinctive of Ephesians is not any individual topic but the way the topics are viewed.

Ephesians is both less and more than a letter. It is less, in one sense, because it lacks the personal references and occasional narrative reflections that characterize letters. Yet it is more, because its essay style permits not merely a more extended exploration of pertinent topics than one might expect in a letter (Paul has done this in letters elsewhere) but also, and more to the point, an architectonic structure. It does contain some epistolary characteristics, but it departs from essay form at significant points. For example, after a modified epistolary opening that identifies the author and recipients and expresses the author's wishes for the recipients' well-being, Ephesians moves into neither a letter nor an essay but a *berakah,* a form of blessing familiar from the Old Testament. The appearance of this liturgical form suggests that we look for other liturgical elements, and we certainly find fragments that have a faint liturgical sound ("to the praise of his glory" or "of his glorious grace" in 1:6, 12, 14), a full doxology in 3:20 and an unmistakable hymn in 5:14.

While it conceivable that such elements reveal a liturgical purpose, at another point Ephesians is far from this when it adopts the conceptual framework of ancient "household codes." It is debatable whether there was a code that was uniform in both form and content, but what appears in Ephesians 5:22—6:9 is certainly distinguishable both in its form and in its content from the surrounding context. In other places there are doctrinal statements, exhortations, prayers and commentary on an Old Testament quotation. Ephesians thus combines a number of literary elements appropriate to the subject matter at hand.

The structure of Ephesians is not unique but is typical of the other letters ascribed to Paul (though not of the Pastorals). Between the salutation and conclusion it contains two major sections. One (1:3—3:21) is doctrinal and includes a benediction and prayer; the other (4:1—6:20) is "practical" (an unfortunate term implying that doctrine is not practical), in the form of an exhortation or paraenesis.

The various features noted above challenge the preacher of today to address the congregation personally (the epistolary aspect), to keep the praise of God foremost (the doxological aspect), to proceed in an orderly presentation of truth (the pedagogical aspect) and, as may be appropriate, to incorporate elements that are familiar to the hearer from both biblical and secular moral literature (the illustrative or supportive aspect). The writer never loses sight of his goal, to present the purpose and plan of God clearly so as to motivate the church to live in a way that will forward that purpose on earth.

☐ Ephesians Among the Letters of Paul: Its Authorship, Destination and Date

The initial observations just made not only help us grasp the essential literary characteristics of Ephesians; they also lead us to questions about the place of this letter among those that are universally acknowledged as Paul's. Such questions are more appropriate to critical exegetical commentaries and need to be addressed in a more comprehensive manner than is possible here. Yet some comments are necessary, especially since this commentary will make frequent specific references to Paul as the author—a position generally held from the early church through most of the church's history.

For many decades debates have addressed such questions as the difference in vocabulary between that of the epistles commonly ascribed to Paul (Galatians, Romans, 1 and 2 Corinthians) and that of those less easily located in his life and work, notably the Pastoral Epistles, 1 and 2 Timothy and Titus. It might be reasonably assumed that whatever difference may exist between Ephesians and the acknowledged works, the fact that Paul's name appears at the beginning as author and is repeated at 3:1, where he describes himself as a prisoner of Christ Jesus, should count as substantial evidence. Yet other portions of Ephesians suggest a different conclusion. The personal note in 1:15 indicating what Paul knew about the readers ("ever since I heard about your faith . . .") can make the reader wonder why the apostle, who spent an exciting two years in Ephesus (Acts 19:10), would describe the faith of the Christians there only in terms of hearsay. Further reflection, however, helps us realize that the Pauline churches grew and declined with sobering rapidity. Galatians 1:6 ("I am astonished that you are so quickly deserting the one who called you . . .") illustrates that, and even the Ephesian church eventually forsook its first love (Rev 2:4). Surely it was important to Paul that he "heard" sometime after his time in Ephesus of the Ephesians' continuing faith and love.

But there is another consideration regarding the lack of personal references one would expect in a letter sent by someone who knows the recipients. Ephesians may have been a circular letter that included Ephesus among its destinations but had to be couched in general terms and could not be specifically directed to those Paul knew in the church of that city.

Observation of such data should precede any judgment regarding authorship. How then should we weigh the doctrinal teaching of this epistle, some of it being characteristically Pauline and some not? The doctrine of justification by grace through faith is certainly a solid part of the teaching of Ephesians (2:1-10) and also of Paul in the epistles commonly agreed to be his. So are the sovereign choices of God (1:3-12), the resurrection and ascension of Christ (1:20-21), the church as the body of Christ and the distribution of gifts for the edification of that body (4:3-16). At the same time there is an expansion on some of these themes, especially regarding the church, that is not typical of other epistles of Paul. The church has a function that transcends its earthly life (3:10-11). Not only does it embrace Gentiles as well as Jews (compare with Rom 11:11-24), but it unites them powerfully (Eph 3:2-6). The writer claims this as a unique revelation to him that goes beyond earlier knowledge (3:5).

The teaching concerning the ministry of the church in Ephesians has struck some as pointing to an author writing sometime after Paul. Romans 12 and 1 Corinthians 12 both list a number of gifts and ministries carried out in the "body," but Ephesians 4:11 lists only five: apostles, prophets, evangelists, pastors and teachers. If "pastors and teachers" refer to a single group, there are only four. Some infer from this that the letter was written at a time when church structure was more developed with a limited group of leaders and, it is maintained, a less charismatic ministry (so-called early catholicism). This issue has been exhaustively discussed, but two facts may be mentioned here as bringing such an early-versus-late schema into question. In the Pastoral Epistles, also claimed to be later, spiritual endowment was conveyed by the laying on of hands along with prophecy (1 Tim 4:14). This is a practice consistent with the charismatic emphasis in the Corinthian letters. Conversely, although 1 Corinthians 12:4-11 mentions a number of spiritual gifts, verses 28-30 of that chapter refer to a limited group of leaders like that in Ephesians 4:11.

Arguments from vocabulary—that Ephesians uses words Paul did not employ in the acknowledged letters—falter when there is allowance for flexibility of style and a recognition of the limitations of statistics. A special circumstance relating to Ephesians is that we have another epistle with significant similarities to Ephesians, namely Colossians. Discussions on authorship must also take into account this comparable material, for a number of scholars who deny the Pauline authorship of Ephesians do accept his authorship of Colossians. There are similarities of structure and of vocabulary such as the following:

Colossians 2:13: When you were *dead in your sins* and in the uncircumcision of your sinful nature, God made you alive with Christ. He forgave us all our sins . . .

Ephesians 2:1: As for you, you were *dead in your transgressions and sins* . . .

Colossians 3:6: Because of these, the *wrath* of God is coming.

Ephesians 2:3: All of us also lived among them at one time, gratifying the cravings of our sinful nature and following its desires and thoughts. Like the rest, we were by nature objects of *wrath*.

Colossians 3:7: You used to *walk [peripatēsete]* in these ways, in the life you once lived.

Ephesians 2:2: in which you used to *live [peripatēsete]* when you followed the ways of this world and of the ruler of the kingdom of the air, the spirit who is now at work in those who are disobedient.

In these examples, similar terms are used in different contexts with similar meaning though differently applied (for example, future wrath against unbelievers in Col 3:6 but unfulfilled wrath against those who became converted in Eph 2:3).

Likewise, similar terms can be used in contexts with different purposes:

Colossians 2:14-15: having canceled the written code [*to . . . cheirographon,* a statement of debt], with its regulations *[tois dogmasin],* that was against us and that stood opposed to us; he took it away, nailing it to the cross. And having disarmed the powers and authorities, he made a public spectacle of them, triumphing over them by the cross.

Ephesians 2:14-15: For he himself is our peace, who has made the two one and has destroyed the barrier, the dividing wall of hostility, by abolishing in his flesh the law *[ton nomon]* with its commandments *[tōn entolōn]* and regulations *[en dogmasin].* His purpose was to create in himself one new man out of the two, thus making peace.

In Colossians the "regulations" are probably the elements of the Old Testament law that were broken and therefore included in the particulars of the statement of debt. These were dealt with at the cross, where also the evil powers were defeated. In Ephesians the "regulations" are either part of the law itself or certain applications derived from the law that tended to separate Jew and Gentile. First one must ask whether in these two epistles that term is used within an acceptable semantic range for one author. It certainly is within such a range, so the question becomes one of application: would one author apply the term in these different ways?

More important, does the author of Ephesians use terms that are similar to those in Colossians but with *meanings* so different that common authorship is impossible? Here are examples involving the word *mystērion*, mystery:

Colossians 1:26: the *mystery that has been kept hidden* for ages and generations, but is now disclosed to the saints.

Colossians 1:27: To them God has chosen to make known among the Gentiles the glorious riches of this *mystery, which is Christ in you,* the hope of glory.

Colossians 2:2-3: My purpose is that they may be encouraged in heart and united in love, so that they may have the full riches of complete understanding, in order that they may know the *mystery of God, namely, Christ,* in whom are hidden all the treasures of wisdom and knowledge.

Colossians 4:3: And pray for us, too, that God may open a door for our message, so that we may proclaim the *mystery of Christ,* for which I am in chains.

Ephesians 1:9: And he made known to us the *mystery of his will* according to his good pleasure, which he purposed in Christ . . .

Ephesians 3:3: that is, the *mystery made known to me by revelation,* as I have already written briefly.

Ephesians 3:4: In reading this, then, you will be able to understand my insight into the *mystery of Christ.*

Ephesians 3:9: and to make plain to everyone the administration of this *mystery, which for ages past was kept hidden in God,* who created

Regarding authorship, among recent commentaries, Andrew Lincoln strongly argues the position that Ephesians is a pseudonymous letter, having moved from his earlier position upholding Pauline authorship (1990:lix-lxxiii). The German Catholic scholar Rudolf Schnackenburg sees it as a later work, on the basis of word statistics, style and theology (1991:24-29). F. F. Bruce approached the issue through a broad treatment of Ephesians with

all things.

Ephesians 5:32: This is a *profound mystery—but I am talking about Christ and the church.*

Ephesians 6:19: Pray also for me, that whenever I open my mouth, words may be given me so that I will fearlessly make known the *mystery of the gospel.*

The word is certainly used in Ephesians with some meanings that are different from those in Colossians. But clearly the word is also used *within* each epistle with differing meanings. And throughout Paul's writings its meaning as well as application varies.

This suggests that it is precarious to draw negative conclusions about common authorship on the basis of differing vocabulary, context, application and meaning. The conclusion that respects the integrity of the letter with its claim to Pauline authorship, its use of Paul's name in 3:1 and its reference to circumstances that presume the author to be Paul in the conclusion (see commentary on 6:21-22) is that the epistle was indeed written by Paul the apostle.

The foregoing discussion has attempted simply to introduce the nature of the issues. Full treatment of authorship can easily be found in Bible encyclopedias, introductions to the New Testament and more detailed exegetical commentaries (see note).

The apparent destination of the epistle was the church at Ephesus in Asia Minor. As noted above, however, questions may be raised by the lack of personal greetings such as one would expect in a letter written to a church known to the author. It was noted above that reasons for this lack can be postulated, including the possibility that this was a circular letter. The words "in Ephesus" from 1:1 do not appear in some respected early manuscripts, including p^{46}, the earliest papyrus containing this letter, and the original hand of Sinaiticus and Vaticanus. There was some confusion as to the relationship between this letter and one to the Laodiceans, at least in the mind of the heretic Marcion. It is significant that although some versions had the words "in Ephesus," the

---

comparable letters in the Pauline corpus (1984:229-46). It is necessary to read his comments in conjunction with his introduction to Colossians in the same volume (1984:28-33). Ten years earlier, Markus Barth had provided a historical survey of opinions and made a clear, though cautious, case against pseudonymity and for Pauline authorship (1974a:36-50). For a good summary of issues, positions and arguments, see Danker 1982.

text used by Origen did not.

Still, it would be hard to explain the fact that the name of Ephesus does appear in other early manuscripts if there were no connection at all with that city. Therefore theories have been developed to explain the circumstances, the most common (and most probable) of which is that the letter was written to Ephesus *and* other churches in Asia Minor. The letter could easily have been carried by a courier, and in this connection the reference to Tychicus in 6:21-22 is important (see commentary). Colossians also refers to him (4:7-9) and to an exchange of letters that Paul requested with Laodicea (4:16). It is reasonable to think that Ephesians could have been circulated as Paul sought to edify more than one church with the majestic truths we benefit from today in Ephesians.

Assuming that Paul was indeed the author and accepting the personal reference in 3:1 as genuine, we need to ask during which of Paul's imprisonments he wrote Ephesians. The circumstances of Philemon, Colossians and Ephesians are similar, suggesting that they were all written during the same imprisonment. Colossians 4:9 mentions that the slave Onesimus would be coming to Colosse with Tychicus, who was carrying the letter to the Colossian church (Col 4:7-8) and the Ephesian letter as well (Eph 6:21-22). These letters seem to have been written when Paul was under house arrest in Rome, following his appeal to Caesar during his trials in Jerusalem and Caesarea (Acts 22—26). Rome would have been a natural place for the runaway slave Onesimus, which is one reason many scholars believe Paul was there at the time of his writing these letters, rather than in Ephesus (where he may have been imprisoned earlier) or in Caesarea (where he was held after his Jerusalem arrest and before being moved to Rome). Based on our knowledge of political history and the transition from Felix to Festus (Acts 24:27), we can assume that Paul wrote Ephesians around A.D. 60.

☐ Theology of Ephesians

1. The Sovereignty of God over the Cosmos From the very first sentence, Ephesians exalts God as sovereign. This in itself is not unusual. In most of his letters Paul maintains that he is an apostle by the will of God. In Ephesians, however, God's will continues as a major theme throughout. According to his own eternal purposes God initiates, plans and accomplishes the multifaceted cosmic agenda by which he will bring blessing to the church, and through it to the entire universe. The commentary on Ephesians 1:3-14 will highlight this by noting the variety of words and grammatical constructions Paul uses to express God's intentions. There is a reprise in 3:10-11 and in his prayer in 3:20-21. This theme is also found in the use of the term "heavenly places," where Christ has ascended to a position over all other beings, notably those hostile to him.

The main picture of God's sovereignty is painted in cosmic dimensions. The focal point is 1:9-10, where the ultimate purpose of God finds expression: "when the times will have reached their fulfillment" and God will "bring all things in heaven and on earth together under one head, even Christ." Everything in time and space will be given meaning—beyond the capacity of any mathematical or scientific theorem to analyze—in the relationship of each part to Christ.

2. The Supremacy of Christ in God's Plan Christ is therefore "over" all, whether one conceives of this in spatial or dynamic terms. In this he leads the way for believers also to be in the heavenly places through their relationship to him (2:6). Believers share this exalted perspective of Christ, from which they can sense the flow of history and their own experiences as part of God's will. They can be assured that being "blessed" by God includes having been chosen by him "before the creation of the world to be holy and blameless in his sight" (1:4). There is not only blessing but also a spiritual goal. This goal has been assigned by the God who "predestined" them "in love" (1:4-5). The appointment to this destiny is not capricious but part of God's intentional plan, which will surely be accomplished (1:11). God's plan is therefore not only cosmic but also personal.

God's plan pertains to the ethical decisions of our daily lives as well. Ephesians 2:10 says that "we are God's workmanship, created in Christ Jesus to do good works, which God prepared in advance for us to do." This ethical dimension of God's plan finds further detailed expression in chapters 4 and 5. Christ himself is the measure of our orthodoxy and maturity (4:13).

3. God's Sovereign Grace In connection with this emphasis on

God's sovereignty, Ephesians focuses on God's wisdom (1:8, 17; 3:10). In addition to this, other attributes of God receive attention, especially his mercy, love and grace. Even here, however, God's sovereignty is important, for it is not only grace but God's *sovereign* grace that is important in this book. The stress in Ephesians on God as the initiator of salvation combined with the portrayal of humanity as dead in sins and helpless to achieve salvation assures us not only that, on the human side, we *need* grace in order to be saved, but also that, on the divine side, God *chose* to be gracious and save us.

4. The Heavenly Realms (1:3, 20; 2:6; 3:10; 6:12) This phrase is important for the understanding of Ephesians. It deserves attention even if for no other reason than that apart from its distinctive use six times in Hebrews and here in Ephesians, the term *epouraniois* occurs in only four chapters of the New Testament (Jn 3; 1 Cor 15; Phil 2; 2 Tim 4). The word carries us up to the sphere that Christ has entered following his resurrection, in which we receive God's blessing, where we share the exaltation of Christ and from which we gain perspective on the role of the church both as it displays God's wisdom to the superhuman powers and as it battles evil forces in that same sphere. The theme of heavenly warfare appears in chapter 6, but already in 1:21 we learn that the ascension of Christ to God's right hand took him "far above all rule and authority, power and dominion, and every title that can be given, not only in the present age but also in the one to come."

5. Mystery The concept of a divine mystery appears at several significant points in Paul's writings, most frequently in 1 Corinthians, Colossians and Ephesians; in the latter book it occurs six times (1:9; 3:3, 4, 9; 5:32; 6:19). God's purposes and plans during the present age cannot be fully known or understood apart from revelation. See especially the comments and note on 1:9, "the mystery of his will." Chapter 3 concentrates on the unforeseen extent to which God would unite Jew and Gentile believers in one body, the church.

6. The Church This church, composed of diverse individuals who are blended into one body in accordance with the mystery of God's plan, is a topic that pervades the entire epistle. The word for church, *ekklēsia,* occurs nine times, mainly in chapters 3 and 5, and the word for body, *sōma,* also appears nine times, all but one of them referring to the church. Although *ekklēsia* does not occur in chapter 4, which may seem strange given that chapter's emphasis on ministry in the church, *sōma* occurs four times there. This points up Paul's conviction that the various believers who minister in the church do so as part of a wonderfully functioning body. The greatest concentration of the two words comes in the passage on wives and husbands, where that relationship is seen to reflect the mystery of Christ and the church.

7. Theology of Ministry This topic is confined to chapter 4, but it is crucial. In Ephesians the nature of ministry grows out of the nature and purpose of the church. Since God not only has reconciled individuals to himself (2:1-10) but also has brought Jews and Gentiles together (2:11-18) and made all believers one growing "holy temple," his dwelling place (2:19-22), and since he has brought all believers into one body (3:1-6) so that God's wisdom can be displayed in the church (3:7-12), Christian ministry must facilitate this ongoing process of assimilation, unity and maturity. This involves doctrinal growth, personal as well as corporate, with Christ as the goal and measure (4:1-16).

Such a goal is achieved by ministry from within the body itself. The people gifted by God are themselves gifts to the church and become equippers of the church, so that ultimately all participate in ministry to one another. Historically the church seems to have often struggled with the implementation of this ideal, so it is all the more important that the ideal be kept firmly in mind.

8. Spiritual Powers and Spiritual Warfare The existence of supernatural beings who seek to exercise spiritual authority *(exousia)* is taught in several Pauline letters. The plural "authorities" occurs four times each in Ephesians and Colossians (Eph 1:21; 2:2; 3:10; 6:12; Col 1:13, 16; 2:10, 15), and the companion term "rulers" *(archai)* is found three times in Ephesians (1:21; 3:10; 6:12) and four in Colossians (1:16, 18; 2:10, 15). Paul stresses the significance both of the exaltation of Christ above all existing spiritual forces and of the continuing battle in which Christians are engaged against them.

9. Prayer Ephesians contains both direct teaching on prayer and examples of prayer. The book opens with a blessing (1:3) which is a prayer of praise to God. Then Paul records two prayers that express his spiritual desire for those who will hear and read his letter (1:15-23;

3:14-21—the latter concluding with a doxology). The commentary will show how these prayers are appropriate to their contexts. The conclusion of the section on the spiritual battle comprises an urgent series of exhortations to pray (6:18-20). This is a necessary expression of Paul's deep conviction that God is at work both in the heavenly realms and on earth to bring about his purposes through the church.

Outline of Ephesians

1:1-2 _____ **Paul greets the recipients of his letter**

1:3-14 _____ **We owe God praise for his great blessings in the heavenly realms in Christ**

1:3 _____ We have been brought into the heavenly realms

1:4-10 _____ Our destiny is part of God's grand plan to sum up all things in Christ

1:11-14 _____ God will work out everything to fulfill his purpose for those who belong to him

1:15-23 _____ **Paul thanks God for all this and prays accordingly for the Christians**

1:15-16 _____ Paul is grateful for the faith and love Christians have

1:17-23 _____ Paul asks God to help believers understand the power of God and the present, exalted position of Christ

2:1-10 _____ **The first step in the fulfillment of God's plan is to raise people spiritually from death to life**

2:1-3 _____ We were in a state of spiritual death

2:4-10 _____ We now have the gift of spiritual life

2:11-22 _____ **The second step in the fulfillment of God's plan is to reconcile Jew and Gentile through the cross**

2:11-12 _____ We were extremely separated from each other

2:13-18 _____ Christ reconciled us to himself and to each other

2:19-22 _____ As a result of this reconciliation, together we form a great temple for the Lord to dwell in

3:1-21_____ The third step is the formation of the church as one body

3:1-6 _____ God's intention is a mystery that is now unfolding

3:7-13 _____ God chose to fulfill his intention through Paul and then through the church

3:14-21 _____ Paul offers a prayer that continues to reveal God's intention in the church

4:1-6_____ The fourth step is to maintain unity in the church

4:1_____ We should live a life worthy of our calling

4:2-3 _____ There are certain personal qualities necessary for our unity

4:4-6 _____ There are certain doctrines that are basic to our unity

4:7-16_____ The fifth step is to foster corporate maturity through God's gifts to the church

4:7_____ Individuality is important

4:8-10 _____ A passage in the Psalms looks forward to the bestowal of God's gifts

4:11_____ There are special gifts—the leaders themselves—whom God has given to the church

4:12-16 _____ These gifts foster both continuing unity and maturity

4:17—6:9 ____ The sixth step is the attainment of Christian morality, accomplished through radical change

4:17-19 _____ Radical change is needed

4:20-24 _____ Radical change has a firm basis in the Christian's life

4:25—5:2 ___ Paul cites specific examples of this radical change

5:3-14 _____ There is a need for still further moral change

5:15-21 _____ We need to be filled with the Spirit

COMMENTARY

In the great art museums of the world, certain paintings stand out because, along with their artistic quality, they are of impressive size. One such is Rembrandt's *Night Watch,* in the Rijksmuseum of Amsterdam. Another is Georges Seurat's *Sunday Afternoon on the Island of La Grande Jatte,* which hangs in the Art Institute of Chicago. Each contains detail that rewards close scrutiny, but each is seen in its grandeur only at a distance.

Ephesians is just such a masterpiece. Its canvas stretches horizontally from "before the creation of the world" (1:4) to "when the times will have reached their fulfillment" (1:10). It reaches vertically from the "lower, earthly regions" (4:9) to "the heavenly realms" (1:3), even "higher than all the heavens" (4:10). Yet this letter contains such precise and colorful detail about God's saving work in our lives and in the church that it requires minute study for maximum appreciation.

☐ **Opening Greetings (1:1-2)**
The Author and Recipients (1:1) Letter writers in Paul's day typically

used scrolls made of papyrus. The recipient of a letter would have to unroll it to discover the sender's name unless the name was put at the beginning. Thus all the New Testament letters that designate an author begin with that author's name, along with some personal characterization appropriate to the contents. Paul sometimes asserts his apostolic authority, an understandable practice when he issues directives. In this case the reference to *the will of God* is particularly appropriate in view of the unveiling of God's magnificent eternal purposes in verses 3-14 of this chapter.

The Christians at Ephesus were probably the first of several churches to receive this letter. Paul calls them *saints* because they have a special relationship to the holy God. This is a common designation of believers in the New Testament, and was also used of God's people in the Old Testament. In Ephesians *saints* occurs also in 1:15, 18; 3:18; and 6:18. Being a saint is not a matter of achievement. Both Romans 1:7 and 1 Corinthians 1:2 address the church as those "called to be saints [or 'holy']." God has called the believers to this position as saints; it is his work, not theirs. They are separated to the Lord. That relationship stands even if, as in the case of the Corinthian church, Christians are worldly and immature (1 Cor 3:1-4). But it is clear that "saints" are to live moral lives (Eph 5:3).

These *saints* are to be *faithful,* a quality that, along with the command to maintain one's "stand" (6:11, 13-14), was important in the cultured pagan cities of that area. The letters to Ephesus and six other churches in Asia Minor that are preserved in Revelation 2:1—3:22 reveal some of the hazards to Christian faith that the believers faced.

The expression *in Christ Jesus* or an equivalent occurs frequently in Paul's writings. It indicates a very close association between Christians

---

1:1 The words *in Ephesus* do not appear in some significant early manuscripts. This fact, along with the absence from the letter of specific references to the Ephesian church, has led many scholars to speculate that this was a circular letter, intended for several churches in western Asia Minor.

Two Hebrew words have been commonly translated "saints" in the Old Testament. One is known from its designation of a pious group in the Maccabean period, the Hasidim. The same name is used today of a strict sect of Jews. The other word comes from the root *qds,* "separated." Where the noun form occurs in the Hebrew Old Testament, the Septuagint uses the word *hagios.* This is the word for "saints" used in the New Testament. (See Gordon 1988.)

and their Lord, a relationship that sometimes is described in terms of incorporation, as in the vivid portrayal of the church as a body of which Christ is the Head. It reappears at several places in Ephesians, notably in 2:4-10.

Salutation (1:2) Ancient letters opened with kind words of greeting. Christian letters "baptized" such commonalties, using such ordinary words as *peace* and *grace* with a Christian meaning that goes beyond mere convention.

The reference to the *Father* as *God,* with Christ mentioned separately, does not deprive the latter of deity. The New Testament tends to employ the term *God* primarily to designate the Father. It usually (though not always) uses other terms for Christ, such as those that emphasize his sonship and his unique earthly mission. This does not impair the identification of Christ with God, but rather focuses on his distinct person and work. At other times God is clearly described as Father, Son and Holy Spirit (see Harris 1992).

□ Celebration of God's Plan and Its Fulfillment (1:3-14)

Jewish literature sometimes couched words of praise to God in a form known as a *berakah* or benediction. It might begin, "Blessed be God . . ." or "Praise be to God . . ." (see Ps 72:18-19). Ephesians 1:3-14 is just such a benediction. The word *bless* could have one of several meanings. Because it could be used both for God's goodness to us and for our thanks to him, it appears reciprocally here: "Blessed be God" . . . *who has blessed us* (v. 3). There is also a semantic extension of this idea in the repetition *who has blessed us . . . with every spiritual blessing*. This reflects an idiom in ancient Hebrew and has an intensifying effect.

1:2 Murray Harris (1992:40-47) provides ample biblical evidence that the New Testament employs the term *God* primarily to designate the Father. He summarizes: "Each strand of the NT affords clear testimony that customarily *patēr,* whether articular or anarthrous, refers to the Trinitarian Father" (p. 271).

1:3 The NIV's *Praise be to* rather than "Blessed is" conveys the proper sense of the word in this context. Unfortunately it loses the semantic pattern "blessed . . . blessed . . . blessing," which is eye-catching in the Greek. See the introduction for more on the *heavenly realms.* For more on Christ's victory over evil powers, see the comments and note on 1:21 and the commentary on 6:10-18.

The word *with* in that phrase represents the Greek word *en,* which occurs three times in this verse. God has blessed us *with every spiritual blessing* (the means by which he has blessed us), *in the heavenly places* (the location of the blessing) and *in Christ* (the source of our blessing). The blessings are called *spiritual,* perhaps to indicate that we receive them through the Holy Spirit or that we receive them as we are filled with the Spirit (compare 5:18), but more likely to distinguish them from material blessings. We do receive material blessings and are thankful for them, and ancient Israel received many material blessings, especially as a reward for obedience (see Deut 28:1-6). God's spiritual blessings, however, reach and touch our inner being, bringing God's loving forgiveness and many associated benefits that infinitely exceed that which is only material. These are recounted in the verses that follow.

The Holy Spirit has a part in this. The blessings have been conveyed by the Father, by the Son and by the Holy Spirit, and the three members of the Trinity are mentioned in that order in verses 3-14. It is the Father to whom the benediction is directed and who initiates, so to speak, the blessings that reach us. Christ and the Spirit are depicted as the agents through whom the Father accomplished his purposes. Note *in Christ* (1:3, 9), *through Jesus Christ* (1:5), *in the One he loves* (1:6), *in him* (1:4, 7, 11) and *through his blood* (1:7). The Spirit is portrayed as a *seal* and a *deposit* (1:13-14). God is fully engaged in our salvation, but that salvation is communicated to us only *in Christ.*

The Heavenly Realms (1:3) God has brought new dimensions into the life of the Christian. This is expressed in two basic ways in the New Testament. One is in terms of the Jewish concept of two ages, present and future. While we are still in the present age, even before certain prophecies of future life and blessing are fulfilled, we enjoy eternal life and the excitement of God's kingdom. In a sense we are already in the new age. This might be called the horizontal dimension. But there is

---

The phrase *in Christ* has drawn much attention. George Eldon Ladd (1974:481-83) provides a brief summary of opinions concerning the meaning of this common Pauline phrase, which occurs eleven times in Ephesians. Donald Guthrie (1981:644-53) sets the phrase in a broader context of Pauline theology. Opinions as to its meaning have ranged

also a vertical dimension. Although we are very much in this world, we also delight in our intimate association with Christ, who has been raised and has ascended to the very presence of God in the heavenly realms. Paul affirms this remarkable fact in two stages: (1) the exaltation of Christ in 1:20-21 and (2) the believer's identification with the risen and ascended Christ in 2:4-7. The effect of this is to give a truly cosmic dimension to the role of Christians and the church.

Similar truths are taught in other letters. Colossians tells us to set our minds and hearts on things above, where Christ is, and indicates that the true source of our life is not here but there, in Christ (Col 3:1-4). Paul told the Christian citizens of Philippi, on whose city and its inhabitants Rome had bestowed cherished Roman citizenship as well as their own, that they were dual citizens in a spiritual sense as well: "Our citizenship is in heaven" (Phil 3:20).

Here in Ephesians Paul emphasizes the heavenly dimension more than in any other letter. After a number of references in the first two chapters, he will refer again to the heavenly realms in 3:10 and 6:12, where he will reveal a remarkable dimension of the church's mission, one that affects even supernatural beings. Paul knew that the church was engaged in an intense spiritual warfare against the world of evil and its manifestations in many areas of life, from "ordinary" sins to magic, occultism, demonic oppression and the direct work of Satan. The place of Christ and the believer in the heavenly realms is not simply a pleasant spiritual idea, but a major factor in the way Christians are to live in such circumstances.

Today's remarkable flow of new information about our physical universe, which should increase our confidence in and awe of God as Creator, may lead others to think of heaven as a distant, irrelevant place with little connection to earth and the visible universe. Ephesians shows that there is a greater universe of space and time than we might imagine. Heaven above and the age to come may exist in a different dimension, but the *heavenly realms* are real and integral parts of God's creation and are presently

---

from a mystical relationship to participation with Christ in a corporate sense. In Ephesians this involves "incorporation into the exalted Christ as [our] representative, who is himself in the heavenly realm" (Lincoln 1990:22).

experientially accessible to Christians, who are *in Christ*.

God's Purpose and Plan (1:4-11) Before examining this passage verse by verse, it will be useful to note some of the special terms here that highlight the forethought, wisdom, plans, purpose and direction of God's activities. Paul uses a combination of strong key words (such as *chosen, predestined, plan* and *will* in v. 11). The idea of purpose is also expressed in the heavy use of various grammatical constructions in the Greek that may not always catch the English reader's eye. Following are some examples.

The words *he predestined us* (v. 5) do not imply that God picked some in order to condemn others. Rather, they show that God did not act in a purposeless way but has a destiny in mind for us. *To be adopted as his sons* (v. 5) articulates the intention behind God's actions. The word *pleasure* in such a biblical context does not merely signify that which makes God happy, but that which he chooses to do. The will of God is not some fatalistic impersonal force but the judicious determination of our all-wise God.

To the praise of his glorious grace (v. 6), echoed in verses 12 and 14, declares not merely some intermediate objective but the ultimate purpose for our existence. The fact that Paul states this three times in this paragraph emphasizes the importance of God's purpose in Ephesians. *With all wisdom and understanding* (v. 8) further explicates the sagacity and care with which God lays and executes his plans. God does nothing thoughtlessly or indifferently. *The mystery of his will* (v. 9) introduces into Ephesians a concept that is found elsewhere in Paul's writings, as well as in other biblical and nonbiblical literature. The word *mystery* was used to convey the wise counsel and purposes of God, which he made known stage by stage. We shall meet it again in Ephesians.

His good pleasure, which he purposed in Christ (v. 9), brings together the related concepts of pleasure and purpose, along with the agency of Christ in the design and fulfillment of God's plans. In *to bring all things*

1:4 Other important passages on God's sovereign acts of choice and predestination are Romans 8:29-33; 9:6-26; 11:5, 7, 28; 16:13; Colossians 3:12; 1 Thessalonians 1:4; 2 Thessalonians 2:13. The fact that choice brings responsibility as well as privilege is evident in Genesis 18:19; Deuteronomy 7:6-8; 10:15-20; 18:1-5; 1 Samuel 2:28; Amos 3:2; John 15:16; Acts 9:15; 1 Corinthians 1:27-28; Colossians 3:12; 1 Peter 2:9.

. . . *together under one head, even Christ* (v. 10), the words *to bring together* render one word in the Greek, *anakephalaiōsasthai,* an infinitive construction that could be understood in more than one way. It could express purpose (that is, God acted in order *to bring* . . .), or it could express content (God's *good pleasure,* that is, *to bring* . . .). Since "God's *good pleasure"* is another way of expressing what he wills, either understanding of that word elucidates the mystery of God's will to reveal Christ as the integrating force of the universe.

Chosen . . . predestined according to the plan of him who works out everything in conformity with the purpose of his will (v. 11) is a summary statement that brings to conclusion this remarkable series of affirmations. Not only does God have marvelous plans, but he accomplishes them fully. The next chapters of Ephesians will show step by step how Christ has brought together such previously inimical groups as Jews and Gentiles—which qualifies him, so to speak, to bring all things into meaningful relationship to himself (1:10) and under his headship (1:22).

The passage magnificently declares that God has wisely determined the best ends for his creation, for his Son and for his people. This means that God's actions in the following chapters of Ephesians cannot be taken as capricious. For example, the principle of salvation by grace, which Paul explains in chapter 2, is neither arbitrary nor offhand. Rather it is in accordance with God's gracious initiative and his ultimate desire for our good and for the glory of his Son. As Ephesians continues, it will expand our understanding of God's purposeful act of salvation to include the unifying headship of Christ over the church, preliminary to the magnificent achievement of 1:10.

The extraordinary proclamation of God's wise purposes in 1:3-14 also means that the reader of the letter is expected not only to learn theology and live properly but also to act with intelligent decisiveness in accordance with these clearly stated divine goals. This is somewhat in contrast to the climate in which today's business decisions are made. The

---

1:5 *Sons* in this phrase seems to be gender-exclusive. It is difficult to translate this masculine term in a way that is both true to the ancient idiom and meaningful today. The term occurs in this context because adoption in Roman society was typically of males rather than of females, sometimes for political reasons. The point is that it was a deliberate choice of a desired person.

remarkable downsizing of IBM in the early 1990s, for example, came about partly as a result of failure to foresee the impending changes regarding personal versus mainframe computers and in the growing market for chips and software. While the church must, of course, be both responsive and proactive with regard to its social environment, the church and individual Christians have the benefit of God's revelation concerning his long-range purposes as they establish their own life plans.

The Believer's Destiny (1:4-5) The time reference for God's act of choosing described in verse 4 *(before the creation of the world)* stresses that this was a decision to which no human being contributed. Paul has a deep sense of God's prerogative in making decisions that affect the destiny of human beings. The word *chose* here is followed by *predestined* in verse 5. In verse 11 Paul uses a Greek word that signifies the choice of heirs, along with a second use of the word *predestined*. The fact of God's initiative in the act of choosing should bring much encouragement to us (compare Is 44:1-2). But the theme of the responsibility that accrues to those chosen is also dominant throughout Scripture.

The single most important object of God's choice is his Servant (Is 42:1), whom we know to be the Lord Jesus Christ (Mt 12:18; Lk 9:35). Most of the national political and religious leaders in Isaiah's day had failed to bring about God's will for his people, so God let it be known that he had designated One who would be his faithful leader. The fact that God chose us *in him* is, as noted above, important and is reaffirmed in verses 6, 7 and 11 (see comments at those points). So is the designation in verse 5 of Christ as the agent through whom God works.

The purpose expressed here for God's choosing us is that we should be *holy and blameless.* Paul's words *in his sight* are startling, since it is God who can scrutinize our hidden faults. It is also God, however, who declares the believer in Christ "righteous" on the basis of the death of Christ for our sin (compare Rom 1:17; 3:21-26; 2 Cor 5:21). It may be, therefore, that Paul has mainly in mind this "imputed righteousness" rather than our character. The imputation of God's righteousness to the believer means that God ascribes or attributes to us that which is not otherwise characteristic of us. This is related to justification, the act of declaring the believer to be without guilt.

This does not mean that character is unimportant. The terms "positional" and "practical" are sometimes used for clarification of this issue. That is, God has put us in a position of blessing in which we have a standing of forgiveness and righteousness. Our salvation waits for a future completion—deliverance from the very presence of sin. This is the "salvation that is ready to be revealed in the last time" (1 Pet 1:5), the eschatological (pertaining to the end times) aspect of our salvation. There is also an immediate practical aspect of God's blessings: deliverance from the penalty and the power of sin. We are already declared blameless in the sense that God has cleared us of guilt, and we are now to live lives that are holy and therefore incur no blame, but we will not be fully *blameless* until the return of Christ.

In several places in the New Testament the idea of blamelessness is associated with the future coming of Christ (1 Cor 1:8; 1 Thess 3:13; 5:23; see also 2 Pet 3:13-14). Also Hebrews 12:14 warns, "Without holiness no one will see the Lord." The final day will reveal who is righteous through Christ, and those people should be careful to conduct themselves accordingly in this present age. While we would not presume to call ourselves blameless or holy, Scripture holds us to high standards. An elder, for example, should have a blameless reputation in society (Tit 1:7; compare 1 Tim 3:2-7). Luke 1:6 describes Zechariah and Elizabeth as following God's commandments blamelessly. This is a way of indicating a disposition to obey God that echoes a number of Old Testament texts, including Job 1:1 and ten other instances in that book. Our responsibility to live holy lives as those chosen by God is stated in forthright language in 1 Peter 1:15-16: "But just as he who called you is holy, so be holy in all you do; for it is written: 'Be holy, because I am holy.' "

In the original New Testament text not only did the words run together, but our present system of verse divisions did not exist. The words *in love* occur without interruption between the words of verses 4 and 5 of Ephesians 1, so it is impossible to know without doubt whether Paul thought of them as modifying the words *holy and blameless in his sight* or *he predestined us*. It may be more proper to connect love with the destiny of sonship described in verse 5 than with blamelessness, an aspect of imputed righteousness.

The occurrence of the word *predestined* here gives no hint of the controversies that would swirl around it in later centuries. Quite simply, in this context it describes the destiny of those who belong to Christ: full sonship. To be *predestined* and to be *chosen* are two distinct but related ideas. When a person is chosen from among others, it is a blessing of God's grace. But this is not only to the benefit of the person concerned. First Peter 1:2 speaks of those "who have been chosen according to the foreknowledge of God the Father, through the sanctifying work of the Spirit, for obedience to Jesus Christ and sprinkling by his blood." One aspect of God's choosing here is "for obedience to Jesus Christ."

There is responsibility connected with being chosen. We have already seen in Ephesians 1:4 that we have a responsibility to be blameless. Predestination in the New Testament has to do with destiny. We are not merely predestined; we are predestined *for* or *to* something, literally "marked out" for something. The present context says we are predestined *to be adopted as his sons* (or "to full sonship"). We have a responsibility to live in a way that honors our adoptive Heavenly Father.

Paul speaks of heirship later, in verse 11. The idea of adoption occurs elsewhere in the New Testament only in Romans 8:15, 23, Romans 9:4 and Galatians 4:5. Adoption was common in ancient Greco-Roman society as a means of bringing a desired person into one's family. The individual was often expected to perform certain services; in one case he was chosen by the emperor to be his successor. The standards of that society made it natural that the adoptee be male, so Paul uses that terminology, but the honor of *adoption as sons* in the Lord's family is bestowed equally on men and women. In the Romans and Galatians passages the greatness of the new relationship is expressed in the emotional address *Abba* ("Dear Father"). There was a sense in which Israel was God's "son" in the Old Testament (Hos 11:1; Rom 9:4), but this relationship did not have the personal significance it has had since the coming of Christ.

The effect of verse 5 is again to evoke praise to God (compare v. 3) for the fact that he truly wanted us and, as the verse concludes, followed his own *pleasure and will* in bringing us into his family. This transcends even the love and expectation with which a family today chooses to adopt a child, wonderful as that is. In Romans 8:19 Paul shows that there is also a cosmic aspect to this, as "the creation waits in eager expectation for the sons of God to be revealed."

Celebration of God's Grace (1:6-8) Christianity offers so much to the individual that it is easy to focus on our benefits rather than on the reason we have received them. The phrase beginning *to [for] the praise of* occurs three times in this section (vv. 6, 12, 14), but only the first includes a reference to God's grace. It is probably assumed in the other two, but in any case focus is on the Giver of grace.

It is improper to consider grace as an independent entity that we can gain and enjoy in itself. Grace is really God being gracious and acting graciously. A parallel to this is love. Love is not an entity in itself, some object that a lover presents to another person. It is the lover loving. So grace is God "gracing." Further, not only is grace the only means of salvation (see 2:8-10), but since God is gracious, it is impossible to approach him on any other grounds. The whole section on God's purposes makes it clear that God takes the initiative in his world, and this includes his bestowal of salvation. We must not picture God as deliberating over several possible means of salvation and deciding on grace. The very nature and purposes of God preclude any other way.

This is emphasized in the following phrase, *which he has freely given us*—literally, "with which he graced us." There is no single English idiom with which to express this verb accurately. It means to bestow grace on someone, showing kindness and favor. The next words, literally "in the one who is in a state of being loved," are meaningfully translated in the NIV *in the One he loves*. This, of course, is God's Son. The point again is that grace, like love, is not some independent entity that can be handed over like a package. It comes to us in, and cannot be received apart from, Christ. Two significant terms of endearment that are applied to Christ in the New Testament are "beloved" and "one and only." God himself employed the first of these at Jesus' baptism, referring to him as "my Son, whom I love" (literally, "my Son, the beloved"—Mk 1:11 and parallels). God reaffirmed his love with the same expression when Jesus was transfigured (Mt 17:5; Mk 9:7). Jesus was also God's "only begotten" Son, or, as we would put it today, his "one and only" (Jn 3:16). The two ideas occur together in the poignant passage about Abraham and his son Isaac in Genesis 22:2. Paul is therefore not using the term "beloved" lightly here.

Verse 7 continues this significant declaration of the source and means of God's grace. As with other aspects of our salvation, it is also in Christ that we have *redemption*. This term often contains the additional idea of payment of a ransom to achieve the desired release. That is why Paul includes the phrase *through his blood*. It cost Christ his life because the *forgiveness of sins,* which appears here in apposition to *redemption,* could be extended to us only when God dealt with that sin righteously. That was accomplished through the death of Christ. A connection between redemption and the forgiveness of sins occurs also in Colossians 1:14 and Romans 3:24-25. The word for *sins* here (literally "trespasses") is relatively infrequent in the New Testament. It seems to be used here with the same basic meaning as the general word *sin* (see commentary on 2:1).

Paul cannot leave the idea of grace; it reappears at the end of verse 7, and he alludes to it at the beginning of verse 8, where he adds to the idea of a free gift the quality of wealthy abundance. Such terminology about wealth reappears in Ephesians 1:18, 2:7 and 3:8, 16. It occurs only twenty-two times in the entire New Testament, but five times in Ephesians, and in connection with different spiritual blessings. This suggests the expansive mood Paul is in as he reflects on all that God is giving us. Perhaps the closest comparison today would be the immense amounts of money offered in the major lotteries and sweepstakes giveaways. Here, though, it is not merely "something for nothing," but an infinity of blessing freely offered. The basic difference, of course,

---

1:7 This is one of the significant verses in the New Testament on the subject of *redemption.* In another frame of reference, 1 Peter 1:18-19 specifies that "it was not with perishable things such as silver or gold that you were redeemed from the empty way of life handed down to you from your forefathers, but with the precious blood of Christ, a lamb without blemish or defect." In Mark 10:45 Jesus uses the word "ransom" to describe the "payment" of his life that was necessary: "For even the Son of Man did not come to be served, but to serve, and to give his life as a ransom for many." Romans 3:24 uses terminology similar to that in Ephesians: "justified freely by his grace through the redemption that came by Christ Jesus." See also 1 Corinthians 1:30; Galatians 3:13; 4:5.

1:9 The Old Testament source for the concept of *mystery* is Daniel 2:18-19, 27, 30, 47, where the Aramaic word *raz* refers to the secret prophecy that God gave the Babylonian king Nebuchadnezzar in a dream. The Septuagint translated this word with *mystērion.*

The New Testament uses include references to the kingdom (Mt 13:11; Mk 4:11; Lk

between this gift and all others is that it is secured only through a relationship with the Giver and that its essence is the priceless intangible of divine forgiveness.

Not only has God given us redemption and forgiveness in accordance with his wealth of grace, but he has given it to us in extreme abundance, as is conveyed by the word *lavished* (v. 8). But this is no impetuous dispersion. God does it *with all wisdom and understanding*. The latter word is a near synonym of the former but may also convey the idea of "thinking ahead." This accords with the basic truth of God's purpose in the universe and for the Christian.

The Grand Plan (1:9-10) At this point Paul unpacks the future, employing an even greater succession of significant words about God's plan. The first verb, *made known,* is not an independent verb standing in isolation, but is linked with the preceding clause about grace abounding. Also the words *with all wisdom and understanding* could, because they stand between the main verbs of verse 8 and verse 9, conceivably point ahead rather than behind and modify *made known* in verse 9. That is, instead of understanding it to mean that he *lavished* all this on us *with all wisdom and understanding,* we would take it to mean that it was *with all wisdom and understanding* that he made the mystery *known* to us. Grammatical technicalities aside, it is impressive how all the terms that come tumbling in abundance out of Paul's mind build on one another to establish a magnificent picture of God's wise plan.

That plan is described as *the mystery of his will.* It is not apparent on the surface, but *mystery* is as significant a term with regard to God's plan as is *will,* if not more so. The Greek term *mystērion* occurs twenty-eight

---

8:10), the destiny of Israel (Rom 11:25), the unfolding of the gospel of Christ (Rom 16:25; compare 1 Cor 2:7; 4:1), the events at the "last trumpet" (1 Cor 15:51), "Christ in you, the hope of glory" (Col 1:26-27), the doctrine of Christ (Col 2:2; 4:3) and the deep truths of the Christian faith—especially the vindication of Christ (1 Tim 3:9, 16). As might be expected, it occurs several times in the book of Revelation (1:20; 10:7; 17:5, 7). The second of these is related to the future consummation of history, when the mystery that was revealed to the prophets will be "accomplished" (10:7; compare "finished," NKJV). This shows that the biblical meaning of *mystery* includes the idea not only of a secret but also of a plan, for one does not "accomplish" a secret.

The term *mystery* can also apply to evil, as in 2 Thessalonians 2:7, the "mystery" (NIV "secret power") of lawlessness, and in Revelation 17:5, 7, the mystery of the symbolic woman, Babylon the Great.

times in the New Testament, over a broad span of books from Matthew
to Revelation. Its connotation is not, as might be supposed, merely a
mysterious secret, but rather God's great plan as he reveals it stage by
stage throughout history.

The word *mystery* occurs six times in Ephesians. This is more, in
proportion to the book's size, than in any other book of the New
Testament (Colossians is close behind). In 3:3-4, 9 it refers to God's plan
of including Jews and Gentiles together in one body, in 5:32 it refers to
the union of Christ and the church, and in 6:19 it refers to the gospel of
Christ. In the present context its deep biblical connotation is clear. It
refers to something God is planning for a future climactic point in history,
when the times will have reached their fulfillment (v. 10, literally "fullness
of times"). This is a significant verse because, like Revelation 10:7, it
shows that history is not a meaningless succession of events.

The NIV clause *when the times will have reached their fulfillment*
includes the idea of an important Greek term without using a separate
word to translate it. The term is *oikonomia,* which some versions
translate as "dispensation." It denoted the management of a
household (which in Paul's day could be large, including an
extended family and slaves), but it also came to describe an
administrative task or arrangement. When Paul wrote of the
"administration" or "arrangement" of the "fullness of times," he
was not thinking merely of a chronological point in history but of
a stage in God's management of history. In this context it does not
necessitate assuming that God predetermines every event individually, but that he manages the whole (compare Rom 8:28).
When this term, *oikonomia,* and others, such as *mystery, will, good
pleasure* and *purpose,* are amassed together, the careful reader is
overwhelmed with the magnificence of God's wise plan in history
and of the place of Christ in that plan.

Paul describes the great act of God at this significant climax of history
with a remarkable and rare verb, *anakephalaioomai.* It has a number

1:10 For the meaning of *anakephalaioō,* see Liddell and Scott 1968:108 and Bauer
1979:55-56. Schlier 1965:682-83 provides examples of its use in literature outside of the
New Testament. Brown 1976:163 has useful comments, including a helpful quotation from
J. B. Lightfoot's *Notes on the Epistles of St. Paul* (1895:322), which says it implies "the entire
harmony of the universe, which shall no longer contain alien and discordant elements, but

of nuances, but here it probably has the sense of summing things up. One example in secular literature is the summarizing of the argument of an orator. Another—seen in the word's only other New Testament usage—is the summation of the Ten Commandments in the one rule "Love your neighbor as yourself" (Rom 13:9). It conveys the idea that all things will be brought into meaningful relationship together under Christ. At present there is fragmentation and frustration. Things do not "add up." On that day, however, under Christ, everything will add up, that is, be summed up in Christ. The idea may be parallel to the reconciliation of all things in Christ described in Colossians 1:19-20.

From here on Paul will demonstrate that Christ is both deserving of and qualified for this exalted position. The church will be the proving ground. God's choice of the believer is therefore not merely an act for individual benefit, but as verse 11 will explain, it is a corporate experience, one that is in accordance with God's plan. The measures that God takes to ensure the destiny of believers (described in the next verses and two chapters) are undertaken with the goal of verses 9-10 in mind.

Paul's process of thought in Ephesians may be accommodated to our own experience if we review our usual procedures in goal setting. When we decide to lay out plans for a project, we usually do several things in preparation. One is to think in terms of the purpose for these plans. (The ultimate purpose of General Motors, for example, is not to give us a sleek car. That is only a means of achieving the company's ultimate purpose, which is to make money.) Once the purpose is clear, we can establish goals and objectives. We will probably write down a series of steps that must be accomplished. We also may list our resources, and perhaps our achievements to date, in order to establish that the goals are realistic. (A projected vacation in the Fiji Islands might not be fiscally possible!) In the process we may note possible hindrances that will need to be overcome.

---

of which all the parts shall find their centre and bond of union in Christ." The root, *kephal-*, is the same as for *kephalē*, "head," which Paul associates with Christ in Ephesians, but it more likely derives its meaning from another word in the group, *kephalaion*, "the main thing, main point, summary or synopsis" (also "capital" in finances; Bauer 1979:429-30).

In the scheme of Ephesians, our purpose is to praise God and enhance his glory. God has established various goals or objectives, the most remarkable one here being the exaltation of Christ described in verse 10. Certain specific and measurable objectives are to be achieved, step by step, toward that unifying reconciliation of the universe under the headship of Christ. One (2:1-10) is the salvation of individuals, which implies their reconciliation to him. Another is the reconciliation of formerly diverse groups of believers to each other (Jews and Gentiles, 2:11-22). A third step goes beyond reconciliation: it is the actual uniting of these previously hostile groups in one body of believers, the church (3:1-12). The next step (4:1-16) depends on us: living a life worthy of the calling that Paul explains in the first three chapters. That step includes maintaining the unity to which God has called us.

Are these goals realistic? Paul's list of blessings already received (1:3-14) should establish that without doubt. We shall see that along with all that Christ has done for us, God has given us his Spirit as a seal and deposit to guarantee the future. But what about hindrances? These have to be taken seriously into account and are described in chapters 4—6. There is doctrinal error that tosses the ship of the church on its waves (4:14); Christian maturity is the answer (4:15-16). There is also the hindrance of old habits, and these must be put away (4:17—5:14). The unity that God wants in the church in advance of the ultimate harmony of 1:10 is produced by God's Spirit (5:15-21). It should especially be found in a Christian home (5:22—6:9). The hindrance that comes from outside is described in 6:10-18, "the devil's schemes." The Christian's armor will halt that assault, as will the Christian's prayer (6:19-20).

In all of this Paul makes it unmistakably clear that Christ is at the center of God's great plans. We have seen this in 1:10. Paul is now ready to show how we fit into God's plans for his Son.

☐ **Inclusion in Christ (1:11-14)** The first words the reader (or, more usually in Paul's day, the hearer) encounters in this section are *in him,* referring to Christ. The effect is not only to reemphasize what has already been taught above about Christ as the source and locus of our salvation but also to link our incorporation into Christ with the grand plan just explained. Paul stresses this further by one more combination of "purpose" terms, this time drawing together tightly our destiny with that of Christ. The statement is in two parts. First is the divine design: *predestined according to the plan of [God]*. Then comes the assurance of completion: *who works out everything in conformity with the purpose of his will*.

This is the second time Paul has used the word *will* (compare v. 5). There is a tendency among Christians to be engrossed in an attempt to determine God's will for each decision in their lives. Many such decisions can be made with more precision and more legitimate reason, however, if they are measured against the long-range will of God that is revealed throughout God's Word. Instead of seeking specific verses for turning points in our lives, we will be far better equipped to make sound decisions if we have a grasp of God's revealed will for the Christian, for the church and for the world. This requires a sweeping understanding of Scripture as a whole. That does not mean we cannot pray for guidance day by day; it does mean that there should be a spiritual maturing in our lives that gives us a solid foundation for making biblically informed decisions.

What Paul is saying here, for example, about our destiny leading to *the praise of [God's] glory* (v. 12) is surely a useful guideline for life's decisions also. In verse 6 God's sovereign actions brought praise to *his glorious grace*. Here in verse 12, Christians themselves (specifically in this instance Jewish believers, signified by *we*) are to be *to the praise of his glory*. The word *glory (doxa)* is related to *dokeō*, to "seem" or to "think." What people think about a person becomes that person's reputation. God's reputation can be enhanced by our thinking more highly of him and by our giving other people reason to think more highly of him also. Since in ancient Hebrew culture the name of a person represented what that person was, we speak of glorifying God's name. To praise God honors him by giving expression to our thoughts about his virtues. The ultimate *redemption of those who are God's possession* (v. 14) certainly will be *to the praise of his glory*, but right now too we can live so as to enhance God's reputation. We cannot enhance what God is, but we can enhance his *glory*.

But something else within this statement calls for careful attention. The verb that is translated *were . . . chosen, klērow,* belongs to a word group relating to the acquisition of something, especially an inheritance. In its earlier history it was used with reference to the casting of lots. We still use the expression "my lot in life." The verb here is passive, so the subject has *become* someone's lot—that is, someone's possession. The translation *chosen* is possible, but there are several reasons for understanding it in a sense closer to the root meaning of the word group, such as "we were made God's portion" or "we were claimed as God's own." (See *The New Testament in the Language of the People* and The Jerusalem Bible. See also Eichler 1976 for further information on "lot" in the Bible.)

One reason for this rendering is that a related noun, *klēronomia,* occurs four times in Ephesians. In 5:5 it clearly refers to the inheritance a person can have in the kingdom. But in 1:18 it refers with equal clarity to the possession the Lord has in his people. In verse 14 it could combine two ideas, our inheritance (the same Greek word) and God's possession. We know that the possession referred to in that verse is God's people, because that possession is said to be redeemed.

A second reason for understanding the verb under question as referring to God's portion is that even though such a concept is not frequent in Paul, it does occur in the Old Testament. While it is true that God can be our inheritance (as was the case with the Levites in Deut 18:2), the reverse is also true. Deuteronomy 32:9 says, "For the LORD's portion is his people, Jacob his allotted inheritance."

A third reason is that the concept of God's inheritance or possession is found elsewhere in the New Testament. First Peter, in a balanced way like that in Ephesians, says both that believers have an inheritance (1:4) and that we are God's special possession (2:9, drawing on Old Testament terminology, Ex 19:5).

This rather extensive concentration on one word is justified by its

---

1:13 It is not possible to determine any temporal relationship between believing and the sealing by the Holy Spirit in this verse. Stanley Porter holds that generally when a participle "occurs before the finite verb on which it depends" it "tends to refer to an antecedent (preceding) action" (1992:188). That sequence occurs here but not in Acts 19:2, where the aorist participle of "believe" *(pisteusantes)* occurs *after* the phrase about receiving

significance in connection with the emphasis in this letter on God's initiative, purpose and grace. It also accords with the three phrases that begin to [for] the praise of (vv. 6, 12, 14). God both gives something to us and gains something in us. In chapter 2 Paul will make a great point that it is not only Jewish believers, referred to in this verse as those who were the first to hope in Christ, but also Gentile believers who are the objects of God's full grace. That truth surfaces already in the present context: And you [Gentiles] also were included in Christ (v. 13). Verse 13 also introduces a strong biblical assurance for those who believed in what is described both as the word of truth and as the gospel of your salvation. Ephesians will later pick up the idea of "truth" in the Christian life (4:15, 21).

The Holy Spirit is involved in two ways to make that possession— both God's and ours—secure. First, he is God's seal on us. The reference is to the ancient practice of identifying and reserving an item, in particular a scrolled letter, for its proper designee. We belong to God, and he has marked us for himself. The seal is the Holy Spirit himself, who indwells the believer. Since there is no grammatical indication that a lapse of time occurs between "believing" and being "sealed" by the Spirit, the soundest assumption is that the use of the aorist tense for having believed signifies the same time as the sealing.

The role of the Holy Spirit is also to function as a deposit (today we might say a "down payment") or as a pledge (v. 14). God will complete the purchase, so to speak, when he redeems his possession, the believer. It is striking that Paul describes the work of the Spirit in commercial terms. While a comparison of the Holy Spirit with a deposit might seem unusual, it drives home the point that God has paid mightily for his possession and will not give it up. While we sometimes (understandably) ponder whether we might lose our salvation, God assures us that he will not lose his possession.

We are learning from Ephesians that our salvation is at God's initiative. If salvation were our work we might have cause to fear losing it. But

---

the Spirit. While receiving the Spirit and being sealed by the Spirit could be different events, that is unlikely. The emphasis seems to be not on the temporal sequence in either passage but on the verbal aspect (completed action). On the matter of verbal aspect see Porter 1989 and the various opinions set forth in Porter and Carson 1993:18-82. See also Dunn 1970.

when the whole process is God's, when he chose to save us, when he made us his possession, we need not doubt that he will carry this through and make sure that he will not lose those who now belong to him.

The reality that we are God's possession, his inheritance, can have a powerful impact on our daily lives. It can deliver us from an overemphasis on how much we receive from God and cause us to realize humbly that we belong to him. That could make us smug, or it can make us sober as we realize that our minds, our desires, our bodies—every part of our being—are not to be pampered and catered to but invested wisely in order to amass the greatest possible inheritance for God.

☐ Paul's Prayer Concerning God's Plan (1:15-23)

Paul breaks into prayer twice in his letter. Perhaps "breaks into" is not quite accurate, for he really slips into it. He begins by telling his readers that he does give thanks and pray for them. He then describes what he prays, and it becomes evident that his heart is directed to God in prayer even as he writes. It is significant that at times Paul records his prayers, sometimes he expresses prayer indirectly (in what have been called "wish prayers"—for example, "May God . . .") and at other times he simply mentions his prayer concerns.

Martin Luther, it is said, actually added extra hours of prayer when his day promised to be long and busy. This is like Paul, who seems to have engaged in prayer far more than one would expect, given the immense expenditure of time required by his missionary and pastoral ministry, his "tentmaking" work to earn support, his letter writing and his travels, which encompassed thousands of miles. It is also striking that although he could address needs and problems with powerful, inspired letters, he did not rely on these alone to accomplish God's work.

In Ephesians Paul punctuates his letter twice with prayers, one here at the end of chapter 1 and the other at the end of chapter 3. Each one is distinctly appropriate to the context. The most obvious instance of this is his reference in verse 18 to the previous themes of hope, calling and inheritance.

Reasons for Thanksgiving (1:15-16) Studies of Paul's prayers and thanksgivings have drawn attention to certain patterns. One of these is the combination of *faith* and *love* (sometimes accompanied by "hope"). Paul often mentions these qualities together, both in prayers and in other contexts (see 2 Cor 8:7; Gal 5:6; 1 Thess 3:6; 2 Thess 1:3; 1 Tim 1:5, 14; 2:15; 4:12; 6:11; 2 Tim 1:13; 2:22; 3:10; Tit 2:2; Philem 5-7; as well as Eph 3:17; 6:23). The combination occurs also in James 2:5 and Revelation 2:19. Faith and love are joined by hope in the familiar love passage, 1 Corinthians 13:13, and also in Colossians 1:4 and 1 Thessalonians 1:3 and 5:8. The impact of all this is clear: the biblical writers, and especially Paul, are concerned with these qualities in the life of Christians. They are both enjoined and praised where they exist.

It is not surprising that Paul is grateful for evidence of the believers' faith in Christ. We may be less prepared for the parallel to this, not love for God but love for other Christians. This does not diminish the importance of love for God, which Paul has stressed elsewhere, but it does raise to prominence our love for other human beings, the second great commandment (see Rom 13:8-10). Paul's use of the terms *faith* and *love* in combination is well established.

The fact that Paul writes *ever since I heard* seems to imply that he did not know the Christians at Ephesus firsthand. This would be consistent with the theory that Paul himself did not write this letter. But if the suggestion noted above is valid, that this was a circular letter, Paul has in mind here the many people in that area of Asia Minor whom he did not know.

Paul's Prayers (1:17-23) Paul combines thanksgiving and petition in his prayers. He also maintains an attitude of reverence in the presence of God, as shown by his use of terms of address (v. 17). In the interest of simplicity and intimacy, we often reduce our address to some simple repeated term, such as "Father" or "Lord." While there is reason and biblical precedence for this, Scripture also supports the careful use of varied and appropriate terms of address to God. In Acts 4, when the disciples were ordered by human authorities to cease preaching in the name of Christ, they addressed their petition for boldness to the "Sovereign Lord" who "made the heaven and the earth and the sea, and everything in them" (Acts 4:24). This was a meaningful way to approach the Almighty, whose great power they now needed.

Spirit and Knowledge of God (1:17) The word *Spirit* in verse 17 could refer either to the spiritual aspect of our learning and being or to God the Holy Spirit, since orthography in Paul's day did not distinguish between capital and small letters. In either case the work of God is needed to bring spiritual understanding, and it is God's Spirit who would accomplish this. The request for spiritual ability to know God better must not be taken to mean that the Bible itself is not clear unless God tells a person inwardly what it means. Anyone—whether a believer or not—with the ability to grasp the syntax and sense of a given portion of the Bible should be able to understand what it is saying. But it takes the inner work (some use the term *illumination*) of the Holy Spirit to comprehend the spiritual implications of the text in a discerning way (1 Cor 2:10-16). Scripture, inspired by the Holy Spirit, is the revelation of God's truth, but true personal knowledge of God himself comes through the *Spirit of wisdom and revelation* in our inner person. Thus while the facts of verses 3-14 are on the page for all to see, the individual's personal response to these facts, and his or her growth in the knowledge of God himself, is a spiritual matter and the proper object of Paul's prayer.

Awareness of the Significance of the Preceding Truths (1:18) This theme of spiritual comprehension continues in verse 18 with the phrase *the eyes of your heart*. Paul uses the metaphor of sight also in 2 Corinthians 4:3-6. Satan has blinded the minds of unbelievers, but God's light shines in our hearts. Unlike our figurative use of the word *heart* to convey the idea of emotion, and unlike the common Christian use of the word to express sincere inward response to gospel truth in contrast to "head knowledge," the Greek word for heart *(kardia)* refers to the whole thinking, feeling and volitional inner person.

There is an echo of our being *enlightened* in an early hymn preserved in Ephesians 5:14, in which sleepers are called to wake up and let Christ shine on them. The object of that knowledge, as mentioned above, is the hope to which God has called us and God's inheritance in the saints. Here again, this involves more than objective knowledge of facts. What Paul wants us to grasp inwardly is something that even Christians have difficulty in realizing.

It was noted above that when Paul writes about an inheritance or possession, he sometimes refers to what we as believers are to receive from God, but he also sometimes refers to what God possesses in us. This verse refers to the latter. Therefore when Paul sets in apposition *the riches of God's . . . inheritance* among us and *the hope to which he has called* us, he is saying that the calling we have is not in this case what we inherit but that which God inherits in us. God considers us a treasure *(riches)!* That to which we are called and on which we are to set our hope is not selfish gain but God's good, which is to the praise of his glory (vv. 6, 12, 14). When Paul tells us in 4:1 to live worthily of "the calling [we] have received," he probably has in mind not so much the work we are called to do or the blessing we are called to receive in heaven, but the share we are to have in bringing glory to God.

Awareness of God's Immense Power (1:19) If all this provides tremendous motivation for us, verses 19-21 also show us the immense power available to us. Typically Paul uses superlatives in describing this power: *incomparably great* (literally, "exceeding greatness of . . .") and then three nouns of overlapping meaning, one meaning active "force" and two that share the sense of "strength" or "might." But even such vivid verbal description is not enough. Paul concretizes this power in two ways. In verse 19 he specifies that it is *for us who believe.* In verse 20 he will demonstrate its accomplishment in the resurrection and ascension of Christ.

While the words *for us who believe* are exclusive, in that nonbelievers cannot draw on Christ's resurrection power, they are not simply expressing some paper benefit to being a Christian. They contain the great spiritual reality that this *incomparably great power* is *like* that which effected the resurrection and ascension of Christ! Although it is not specified in this section, we also know that if the Spirit of Christ (3:16-17) truly resides in our hearts, he is the *same* Christ who was raised from death, the same Holy Spirit "who raised Jesus from the dead . . . living in you" (Rom 8:11). Romans goes on to say that "he who raised Christ from the dead will also give life to your mortal bodies through his Spirit, who lives in you."

We must never underestimate the power of God that resides in the believer when we need help in temptation, power in prayer, boldness in witnessing or courage to do what is just and right. This is not a power at our disposal; it is for God to exercise to accomplish his will. Obedience opens the way.

Awareness of God's Power in the Resurrection and Ascension of Christ (1:20-21) Great as God's power was proved to be in the resurrection, in the ascension we see that power bringing Christ into the position of ultimate honor at the *right hand* of God, from where his authority is extended over all beings, specifically all the forces that could conceivably challenge Christ for supremacy (v. 21).

Among other things, the way Paul describes the power necessary to do all this makes it clear that he knew the resurrection and ascension to be actual events (v. 20), not myths or merely "spiritual" concepts. Further, Christ did not rise into some ideal but unreal world but to *the heavenly realms,* where in his position of honor with God he is over hostile beings who are also real and who challenge him for supremacy. These *heavenly realms* were mentioned in 1:3 and will be mentioned again in 2:6 as the place of the believer enjoying the blessings of God. In 3:10 as in 6:12 these realms are the place of God's active sovereignty over unseen forces, and that is the case here in 1:20.

The emphasis on our Lord's ascension in Ephesians is in accord with its importance elsewhere in the New Testament. As early as chapter 9 in Luke's Gospel there is a reference to his approaching ascension (v. 51, where the word for "taken up" is the same as one of the words used in Acts 1 to describe the event). One might have expected Luke to mention the cross or the resurrection as the climax of Jesus' life, but instead he looks beyond these to the ascension. In fact, there is even a foreshadowing of it in the Old Testament, where in Psalm 110:1 the Lord says to David's Lord (the Messiah, as Jesus made clear—Mt 22:41-46 and parallels), "Sit at my right hand until I make your enemies a footstool for your feet." Psalm 110:1 is quoted and alluded to several other times in the New Testament (for example, Heb 1:13), which shows the importance of Christ's ascension to the right hand of God the Father. Romans 8:34 alludes to it and tells us that Christ is presently interceding for us at God's right hand. (This intercession is accomplished by the

---

1:21 Two works in particular on the supernatural power struggle in the heavenly realms

presence there of the One who died for us. That presence is in itself a plea before God on behalf of our complete forgiveness.) Therefore, while there is some truth and much feeling in the lines sometimes sung at Easter, "You ask me how I know he lives? He lives within my heart," that pales in comparison with the fact that Christ lives at the right hand of God, where he intercedes for us and from where he will oversee the defeat of his enemies.

These enemies are not simply earthly authorities, as has sometimes been supposed, but supernatural forces. The prominence in Ephesians of such themes as the existence of opposing forces, the reality of spiritual warfare and the believer's powerful resources needs to be taken more seriously than has often been the case. There are four ways in which the forces mentioned in 1:21 and in 3:10 have been understood: (1) supernatural forces, without differentiation between good and bad, (2) evil supernatural forces, (3) mythological forces (that is, the *concept* of [usually] evil rather than actual beings—a process of thought that began already in ancient times) and (4) evil human rulers. The human rulers can be seen as led by actual evil forces (2) or that category can be thought of as a consequence of the concept of evil (3).

The contexts in Ephesians where Paul refers to such beings are best understood as describing not human powers but divine, not mythological forces but real. That is so in the passages just mentioned, 1:21 and 3:10, and also in 6:10-18, where they are clearly evil. That raises the question whether the forces mentioned in 1:21 and 3:10 should be in category 2 rather than 1.

There are two basic approaches to this question. One is to consider that not only do the forces named in Ephesians have an evil character at least once, but also there is a mass of evidence in ancient literature, Jewish and pagan, especially in the magical papyri, that powers not otherwise identified might be considered evil. In fact, forces that are "named" (as here in 1:21) are typically invoked or controlled in magical incantations. If this has the import that it seems to, the NIV misses the connection with the translation *every title that is given*

---

deserve careful study: Arnold 1989 on Ephesians itself and Arnold 1992 on this and related themes in all the Pauline letters. See also Roberts 1993.

(compare NRSV's "every name that is named"). The other approach is to assume that some of the terminology (or "names") used in 1:21 and 3:10 may refer to benign beings, such as angels. The hermeneutical principle would be to let the context control whether they are considered evil or not.

A reasonable conclusion may be that as Paul wrote Ephesians he was careful to establish the exaltation of Christ without at first identifying the powers as evil, though he must have known this would be in the readers' minds. The superiority of Christ was then specified as a victory over evil powers in which the believer shares, taking the side of the mighty Warrior already known to Jewish believers from the Old Testament.

Awareness of the Headship of Christ over the Church (1:22-23) Paul's words assure us that the ascension carried Christ far above whatever other beings can be conceived of, not only in but also beyond this universe. He alludes again to Psalm 110:1, this time to stress the defeat of the Lord's enemies. In a further step Paul introduces the terms *head, church* and *body* (that is, the church, of which Christ is the head). The meaning of *head (kephalē)* must be determined by its context, because when used figuratively in the ancient world it had more than one meaning. It was a symbol of prominence (the rest of the body was covered up, while the head was clearly visible) and honor (in contrast to the feet; see 1 Cor 12:21-24, where the usual attitude to certain parts of the body is contrasted with the attitudes Christians should have to each other). It could also convey the idea of source. Ancient physicians are known to have had the idea that bodily fluids originated in the head. Another figurative use expressed the idea of rulership, although this was not nearly as common as has been thought. (See note on 4:15 for a survey of studies on *kephalē*.)

In the present passage the word seems to have the third use, rulership. Its meaning in 4:15-16 and its significance in 5:23 are debated and will be discussed at those points. As for the word *head* in some English translations of 1:10 *(to bring . . . together under one head),* this word occurs in the Greek text not as a noun but as part of a verb, probably meaning "to sum up." (See note on 1:10.)

In the present passage not only is Christ head over everything, but he has this position for the benefit of the church. (We shall see the significance of the church in the coming chapters, as well as the use of the term *body* to describe it.) Paul has now gone beyond his actual prayer to enlarge on the meaning of his petitions. In so doing he has given us a rich and wonderful insight into the present exalted position of our Lord.

Just as it is possible, when hiking through mountainous areas, to devote so much attention to finding the right trail, observing the compass, studying the geology of the area, learning statistics about elevation and so on that we miss the beauty of the peak, so one can study this marvelous, exegetically intricate passage and miss the wonder of the person of Christ. Perhaps we do not think of Ephesians as much in christological terms as we do its sister epistle Colossians, but the doctrines of salvation and the church that characterize Ephesians are dependent on the truth about Christ. His exaltation as described in the first chapter is worthy of our focused attention. The terminology, the grammar and the sentence structure, while essential to the pursuit of exegetical and theological trails, should lead us to lift our eyes to the theological summit, the Christ who has been exalted above every conceivable name and being.

☐ Step One in the Fulfillment of God's Plan: The Great Transition from Death to Life (2:1-10)

There is no greater contrast in human experience than that between life and death. Physical death means the cessation both of personal relationships and of personal experiences on earth. Spiritual death means personal and experiential separation on the spiritual plane. The person who is "dead in sins" has neither a spiritual relationship with God and believers nor a personal experience of spiritual things.

Several further introductory comments on spiritual life and death may be useful. These reflect the general teaching of Scripture, with special reference to John 5:24-30. At the beginning of that passage Jesus' words are "I tell you the truth, whoever hears my word and believes him who sent me has eternal life and will not be condemned; he has crossed over from death to life. I tell you the truth, a time is coming and has now come when the dead will hear the voice of the Son of God and those who hear will live" (vv. 24-25). Clearly, physical death ends a previous experience of physical life and in that sense is an event, while spiritual death is a state in which all human beings exist unless given spiritual life. Furthermore, according to Jesus, a believer who dies physically will live forever spiritually and will also participate in the future resurrection; an unbeliever who dies physically while still in a state of spiritual death remains in that state and has no hope of resurrection to life. We are all dying physically and cannot by simple choice reverse that direction; we have all been dead spiritually, but by receiving God's grace in Christ, can turn from death to life.

At creation God breathed the breath of life into the human being he had made (Gen 2:7), but at our conversion God makes us alive in Christ. This second breath of God is usually only dimly understood by believers, let alone by those who do not yet have spiritual life (Jn 3:5-8). It is God's work by grace. Ephesians 2 takes us from spiritual death to spiritual life.

The State of Spiritual Death (2:1-3) *As for you . . .* The emphatic opening to this chapter could not have failed to arrest the attention of the original hearers, especially the Gentiles among them, as they heard it being read. Previously Paul had written about both "us" and "you" (presumably Jews and Gentiles) as those included in God's blessings. Now, in order for the recipients, especially those who were Gentiles *(you),* to understand the meaning and significance of their new spiritual life, he must speak bluntly about their previous state of spiritual death and its causes.

Existence prior to receiving eternal life is not, as might be supposed, a state of neutrality. Such an assumption would be to ignore Paul's vivid, devastating description of the spiritually dead as being in sin and under satanic dominion. Those who have not yet entered life are destined for judgment (Jn 5:24), a state that is described here as being *objects of wrath* (Eph 2:3). The term *transgressions* is probably used here as an approximate synonym for *sins,* the use of two terms adding emphasis but not signaling a difference of meaning. They were distinctive terms, but by the time of the New Testament they could be used synonymously. One example of a place where these two terms express the same idea is Romans 5, where "sin" in verses 12-13 is followed by "transgression" (NIV "trespass") in verses 15, 17 and 18 and the reappearance of "sin" in verse 21, without any apparent change in meaning. The Lord's Prayer also provides an example of the synonymous use of terms for sin. "Debts" *(opheilēmata)* in Matthew 6:12, "trespasses" *(paraptōmata;* NIV "sins") in Matthew 6:15 and "sins" *(hamartias)* in the parallel in Luke 11:4 seem to be used without any difference in meaning.

The expression translated *in . . . sins* (Eph 2:1) may refer to a sphere of existence, though the NRSV may be right with "through . . . sins," which indicates means or causation. Either way, the idea of sphere becomes clear in the next verse, which begins with *in which.* It is probably inaccurate to think of all non-Christians, though blinded (2 Cor 4:4), as being under satanic control directly. Nevertheless verse 2 shows that non-Christians, whether consciously or unconsciously, are conforming to the world in which we live.

Followed the ways of this world (v. 2) is literally "walked according to the age of this world." "Age" *(aiōn)* and *world (kosmos)* are overlapping terms. Paul often combines similar terms by putting the second one in the genitive case ("purpose of his will" in 1:11) or even a second and third term (literally "working of the might of his strength" in 1:19). "Age" is primarily temporal; *world* is spatial. Together they describe a godless culture and society.

Paul's consciousness of the spirit world "above" the physical one, which is especially clear in Ephesians, appears here also as he writes of the evil one who rules *the kingdom of the air. Kingdom* is one way to translate the Greek *exousia,* "authority." It is power in the sense not of force but of a personal influence by which one controls others. One might think, on a lesser scale, of cult leaders who exercise unbelievable control over their compliant followers. Paul uses an idiomatic expression (literally "sons of disobedience") to describe those who follow this evil ruler as people who are characterized by disobedience. Obedience to the wrong ruler of course means being in a state of disobedience to the right one. Worse, this spirit is actually at work right now in people's lives.

This is a frightening thought, but even more so as Paul reminds us that we all (even sincere religious people as Paul had been) were in this situation. He then proceeds to describe what it involved. First we note that two different verbs are translated *live* in these verses. In verse 2 it represents the Greek word for "walk" *(peripateō)*, which connotes a way of life ethically viewed. In verse 3 it represents a word for "conduct" *(anastrophē)*, a way of life and behavior.

The *cravings* (v. 3) we all experience are localized in *our sinful nature* (the "flesh"—*sarx*). The televised sex and violence that concern many today portray the lack of self-restraint in our society, expressing what Paul calls the "flesh." Paul uses this term frequently (but not solely) with a negative ethical content, as in Romans 7—8 and Galatians 5—6. Here in verse 3 it describes the terrible inclination to sin that drives human beings. The Revised English Bible tries to get the idea across by using the phrase "physical passions."

Christians have sometimes thought of the body itself as sinful. Paul, however, sees the parts of the body as potential "instruments" either of sin or of righteousness (Rom 6:13). While the semantic range of the word "flesh" is so broad that the term can mean the physical body in a literal sense, "flesh" also refers to the nonmaterial *sinful nature,* the source of evil in us that finds expression in our physical flesh or body. So in verse 3 Paul speaks of the *desires and thoughts* of the flesh.

This reference to *thoughts* may indicate a further deliberate inclination or process of imagination in addition to our base impulse to sin. In Romans 7 the inner being approves God's law but is powerless to produce obedience. Romans 1:28 shows that human reasoning is distorted by sin. The "flesh" or *sinful nature,* which in Romans 7:23 is the agent by which we serve sin, here in Ephesians is that which motivates us to sin. In this condition we human beings have incurred God's proper anger, not merely because of specific acts of sin but because we are in this state "by nature."

2:3 It is difficult to translate the Greek word *sarx* (NIV *sinful nature*) because both that word and its common English counterpart, "flesh," have such a range of meanings. Both have figurative meanings. Shakespeare's famous expression "pound of flesh" is one English example. Among the literal meanings, some are common (a "flesh wound"), while some are specialized and not often heard, such as "fleshfly" and "fleshhook." On the border between literal and figurative one could place the familiar biblical words "The spirit is willing but the flesh is weak." Here "flesh" represents the body as opposed to the spirit, but it is broader than the physical skin and such, referring in general to physical ability. In Paul the term can refer to the evil aspect of our persons, which is often connected with physical senses and deeds and yet is not bad simply because it is associated with the body and its functions. The term "works of the flesh" can mean bad things that people do when

The NIV translators' use of *wrath* instead of "anger" helps to distinguish the deep righteous anger God has against evil from sinful human outbursts. Romans 3:5 makes it clear that God is not unjust in bringing his wrath on us, because otherwise he could not judge the world. The same word appears in the graphic description of the final struggle between God and evil in the book of Revelation (6:16, 17; 11:18; 14:10; 16:19; 19:15). *Objects of wrath* represents a Semitic idiom, "children of wrath," preserved in the NRSV, indicating that wrath is one's destiny. (Compare the similar idiom "sons of . . ." which in v. 2 indicates a characteristic.) Such terminology is usually paraphrased in modern versions, but it is vivid and its force needs to be recognized.

The Gift of Spiritual Life (2:4-10) As I was revising this section, during the Christmas season, word came of a little girl who was rushed to the hospital with a potentially fatal disease. Naturally, Christmas gifts became immediately inconsequential to that family. At such times we are reminded that life is important beyond all comparison with anything else. Sadly, in contrast, when the precious gift of spiritual life is offered to people in spiritual death, the response is often simply to return to their toys. This calls for God's mercy and grace.

Verse 4 begins *But . . . God . . .* This focuses on God as the one who intervened in our desperate circumstances. The conjunction *but* has an adversative sense here—that is, it introduces a contrast. God is *rich in mercy.* This is unexpected, because of the reference to wrath in the preceding verse. It calls to mind the prayer of Habakkuk, "In wrath remember mercy" (Hab 3:2). The mercy of God is one among several focal points in Paul's contrast between spiritual life and death. It is

moved by evil desires.

When Paul says that we were children of wrath *by nature,* our "natural" inclination is to wonder whether this is not unfair. Why should God have anger toward those who are the way they are through birth and not by individual choice? The word *nature (physis)* is not the same word or idea as *sinful nature,* the NIV translation of the Greek *sarx,* "flesh." It could be translated "by birth," as in the NIV translation of the similar word in Galatians 2:15, "We who are Jews by birth." Paul does not explain here what this means or what its connection may be with Adam and "original sin." He seems to be making the point that we are not simply people who practice sin, we *are* sinful; yet we are responsible for acting out that sinfulness rather than repudiating our sinful tendencies.

possible for the reader to concentrate so closely on the rich proliferation of descriptive words in this section that the overarching theme of life and death is forgotten. As the chapter progresses the contrast will widen to include a chronological dimension (then and now) and what might be called a spatial dimension (away from God and near God).

This Life Is by Grace (2:4-5) Several significant terms are brought together in this paragraph: *mercy, love* and *grace.* To say that God is *rich in mercy* continues the characteristic way of Ephesians in describing his generosity as he distributes his spiritual resources. The adjective *rich* occurs here instead of the noun "riches" (or "wealth") used in 1:7, 18; 2:7; 3:8, 16. God has saved us first (in the Greek word order) because of his mercy and second because of his love (2:4). *Great* modifies the word *love* in something of a parallel to the idea of the "wealth" of mercy. Through the use of an awkward-sounding Greek idiom, "his love which he loved us," Paul shows that God's love is active, not merely abstract. It is also undeserved. Deuteronomy 7:7-9 shows that God did not set his affection on his people because of their achievements but because of his love for them.

This love is, in turn, related to that faithful love that can be described as God's merciful and gracious covenant loyalty (Hebrew *ḥesed*). (Compare Is 63:7 for an example of this word [there translated "kindnesses," plural, in NIV], where it is paired with the word for "compassion.") In the New Testament this kindness or covenantal faithfulness is best represented in the word *grace,* which first occurs here in verse 5. In ancient times that word had a range of meanings that expressed in one way or another the idea of a capable person voluntarily doing something for the well-being of a less capable person. Paul's use of

---

2:5 Paul does not explain here what *made us alive with Christ* means. A study of other passages such as Romans 6:1-14 is necessary for a full understanding. The phrases *raised us up with Christ* and *seated us with him* (Eph 2:6) cannot mean that we have experienced the same physical resurrection and ascension that Jesus did, but clearly there is a spiritual experience that corresponds to those. That does not minimize the reality that because Christ is alive again after death, somehow we also have received new life in union with him. It is clear that one day we shall also experience a transformation that affects our whole corporate being, not just our inner spirit (1 Cor 15:35-58).

For Paul *grace (charis)* is "the essence of God's decisive saving act in Jesus Christ, which took place in his sacrificial death, and also of all its consequences in the present and future (Rom 3:24ff.)" (Esser 1976:119). The role of grace is an important issue in

grace (charis) in turn has additional qualities of meaning.

In between the paired words *mercy* and *love* and the word *grace,* Paul picks up (v. 5) some of the wording of verse 1 about being dead in transgressions and then states the contrast: God *made us alive with Christ.* The NIV reverses the order of the death and life phrases for smoothness, but loses the chronological impact in so doing. The NRSV inserts "together" before "with" to convey the force of the Greek verb, which means to "make alive together with [someone]." This verb finally completes the thought Paul had in mind when he began this section in verse 1. In between there is a series of participial and relative clauses, all subordinate to the coming main verb and all maintaining the suspense.

Paul does not go on to explain just how we are made alive with Christ but instead moves to God's grace as the reason, along with his mercy and love, for this wonderful fact. The words *it is by grace you have been saved* will be repeated in verse 8, but by inserting them here Paul not only introduces the idea of grace but also identifies the resurrection of Christ as a saving work. For the first-century Jewish reader or hearer, salvation was a frequent and wonderful act of God in Old Testament times by which he intervened in the life of his people at crucial moments and rescued them from disaster. People were saved from military defeat, from other threats to personal health, from danger of various sorts and from spiritual ruin. (See Liefeld 1988:287-95 on the meaning of salvation in both Old and New Testaments.)

Both terms, *grace* and *saved,* therefore assume (1) the ability of the donor and (2) the need of the receiver. No need is greater than spiritual death, and no act since creation is greater than the resurrection of Christ.

Protestant and Catholic theology, and Schnackenburg's commentary on Ephesians at this point is helpful for understanding the classical Roman Catholic teachings on salvation. He suggests strongly on the basis of Colossians 2:12-13 that "the change from death to life . . . refers to the event of Baptism" and that "Baptism is also in Eph. the fundamental event in salvation" (Schnackenburg 1991:94). It should be noted that Ephesians mentions baptism only in 4:5, "one Lord, one faith, one baptism." Further, regarding 2:8-9 Schnackenburg holds that "faith does not stand as an emphatic antithesis to works" in spite of the words there, *For it is by grace you have been saved, through faith . . . not by works.* He interprets this with regard to "the temptation to self-praise" over our "achievements" facilitated by grace (v. 9; Schnackenburg 1991:97). Nevertheless, his comments throughout this section are strongly christological.

To be made alive with him, then, is truly salvation by grace.

This Life Is for a Purpose (2:6-10) The truth of God's eternal purpose and plan resounds throughout Ephesians. Here in 2:6-10 there are three purpose clauses. God's purpose includes, on his part, showing us the wealth of his grace in coming ages (v. 7) and then, on our part, not boasting (v. 9) but doing good works prepared by God (v. 10). This introduces a sense both of anticipation and of responsibility. The same Greek grammatical construction is used for each, so the force of this was more obvious to the original readers (or hearers) than to readers of most modern versions, which tend to vary the wording for the sake of style. Literally it is "in order that he might show" (v. 7); "in order that we might not boast" (v. 9) and "in order that we might walk in them" (v. 10).

When verse 6 picks up the reference to the resurrection of Christ (1:20) by saying that we have been *raised . . . up* with him, it builds on a fundamental fact central in early Christian preaching. This fact is that Jesus was not only resurrected but also raised to a position of exaltation (see Acts 2:32-33; 5:30-31). The climax of that exaltation was the seating of Christ at the right hand of God. Now a totally unexpected and remarkable truth emerges: the believer not only has been given life with Christ but has been linked with Christ in his ultimate exaltation at God's right hand. Further, the term *heavenly realms,* which occurred at the beginning of this letter (1:3) as the sphere of God's present blessing of the believer and then in Paul's first prayer (1:20) as the sphere of the present exaltation of Christ, now appears again as the sphere of the believer's new life with Christ. All this takes place *in Christ Jesus* (compare *in Christ,* 1:3, 20). This typically Pauline expression serves here to emphasize the union experienced by the believer and Christ in their exalted position.

This revelation that the Christian's spiritual experience parallels the spiritual/physical experience of the resurrected Christ is nothing short of amazing. The entire Ephesian letter is shaped, in fact, by this picture of victory and exaltation. We shall see the way God is celebrated in the heavenly realms (3:10-11) and how the present life of the Christian is

---

2:7 For the idea of God's *riches,* see 3:8 and comments, and for God receiving glory

energized by the interrelated truths of God as superior divine warrior and of Christ as superior to all hostile forces (6:10-17).

An English class I took at university was held in a room that faced a building under construction. The noise dulled the senses, and on one particular day was supplemented by darkening skies that made the class all the more depressing. Suddenly my attention was arrested as the professor began discussing the concept of heaven. His words, which penetrated through the noise and heavy classroom atmosphere, come to mind every time I read verse 7 of this passage: "Heaven must be a boring place." If God, *in the coming ages,* is going to *show the incomparable riches of his grace,* how can heaven be boring? This overshadows all stray thoughts about what heaven will be like. Such questions as "Will my pet dog be in heaven?" or "Will they play Bach?" or even "How will I recognize my loved ones?" recede into the background when we contemplate the prospect of God, throughout the ages to come, displaying his *grace, expressed in his kindness to us in Christ Jesus!* Even this is not only for our pleasure; it is a demonstration to all who observe God's wealth of grace. Monarchs display the contents of their treasuries and millionaires parade their luxury cars, but God's display is of his kindness.

This Life Comes by Grace Instead of Works (2:8-10) There are few verses both more important and more misunderstood than 2:8-9. This is partly because verse 10 is often not quoted along with them. When I was a young Christian I acquired a pack of Bible verses to memorize. Among the first were Ephesians 2:8-9. I began quoting them in witnessing, but it took me years to realize that the omission of verse 10 was one reason I was having trouble persuading my morally sensitive friends that salvation is only by grace. The almost inevitable response was that if this is true, Christians can live as they please and still go to heaven. Romans 6:1 deals with this issue as well, but when we quote Ephesians 2:8-9 it should not be necessary to leave the Ephesian context, because verse 10 gives the needed corrective: we are *created in Christ Jesus to do good works.*

The meaning and importance of salvation by grace were explained

---

through the demonstration of his character and works, see 3:10 and comments.

in connection with verse 5 above (see comments and note on that verse). Verse 8 adds that it is *through faith*. The word *faith* occurs seven other times in Ephesians (1:15; 3:12, 17; 4:5, 13; 6:16, 23). Given the context, faith is the means by which God's grace is accepted and cannot be understood as contributing to salvation in any sense. Although Christ is not mentioned as the object of faith in verse 8, that is clear elsewhere in the New Testament (for example, Acts 16:31; Rom 3:22). Even in Ephesians, however, the nuances of meaning vary. Faith is one of two characteristics Paul considers important as identifying Christians, along with love (1:15). We may tend to think of faith mainly as an act at a particular time, a response to the gospel that is necessary for salvation. It is truly that, but like the love with which it is paired in 1:15, it is not a one-time event. Love is ongoing and (one hopes) growing. Those vital characteristics should mark faith also.

Faith is also the way we maintain a continuing healthy relationship with God. "In him [Christ] and through faith in him we may approach God with freedom and confidence" (3:12). In that context Paul is speaking of his mission to make known the mystery of God, confident that sufferings will not deter him from that mission. We do not come to God thoughtlessly, even though the way has been opened through Christ, but we do it consciously by faith in him, realizing that apart from such faith we do not have that "freedom" or "confidence." Faith helps us keep our awe of God and our appreciation that we now have the right to come to him.

Later in chapter 3 the picture changes from our coming to God to Christ's dwelling in us. Paul prays "so that Christ may dwell in your hearts through faith" (3:17). A man came to our church in answer to his mother's prayers, neither of them knowing that I, a friend of his mother, was serving there as a pastor. Subsequently he and his fiancée, now his wife, experienced spiritual awakening. He evidenced new stages of understanding and faith. Yet in spite of the changes and even though he sought to bring others to Christ, there was something missing. He has just told me that he has come to realize that he needed to allow

---

2:8 "The words 'and this does not proceed from yourselves; it is God's gift' are probably to be taken as parenthetical, inserted into the statement that salvation is received 'through faith, . . . not on the basis of works.' Interpreters have differed on the precise reference of

Christ to come in and fully occupy his life. I believe that Christ is now "at home" in Dave's heart. At which stage was he born again? I do not know, but it is clear that faith has been operating in his life and has certainly been the means of Christ's "dwelling" in him.

As I write this, near an airstrip in the north woods of Wisconsin, a small single-engine plane is taking off. It has taxied down the runway and is now airborne, heading into a cloudless sky. "By faith" the pilot decided to commit him or herself to that plane's structure and operational facilities; by faith he or she started the engine, by faith taxied down the runway to the point of no return and now, by faith, is resting in the unseen aerodynamic forces that support plane and pilot. Perhaps that last (and lasting) "rest" can be compared to the faith Dave now has, resting in the indwelling Christ.

In Ephesians 4:4-5 a significant change takes place in the meaning of "faith." "There is . . . one Lord, one faith, one baptism": faith here is more than our individual response to God. In 4:13 it is "the faith" and refers to the whole truth revealed by God, accepted by believers and maintained by the church. From trust in the Lord to an ongoing relationship with him to what we corporately believe about him, faith is essential.

Therefore when we learn in 6:16 that faith is to be our shield against the evil one, we know that this is not merely a momentary response to an evangelistic appeal but the whole of our ongoing response to God, relationship with him and confidence in what he has taught us. It is not surprising that when Paul gives his closing benediction of peace in 6:23 he mentions together, as he did in 1:15, those ongoing Christian characteristics of "love with faith."

To what does *this* refer in the phrase *this not from yourselves* (2:8)? It could refer to *faith,* the immediately preceding word, although its grammatical gender is feminine, while the gender of *this* is neuter. Possibly it refers back to *grace,* though on several counts that is unlikely. It is most probable that it refers to the whole saving work expressed in verse 8. All this is truly *the gift of God. Not by works* (v. 9) is the antithesis

---

'this.' If the Greek pronoun were feminine, agreeing in gender with 'faith,' then the reference to faith would be plain. The sense would be: even the faith through which you have been saved is not your own doing; you could not have exercised it unless God had given it to

of verse 8. The two, *grace* and *works,* are mutually exclusive. In Galatians and Romans, when Paul writes of "works" he often refers to them as "works of the law." Romans 3:28 is a typical and important example of this. He also explains that since works are excluded from the process, we cannot boast (Rom 3:27; 4:2). All glory must go to God—a prominent theme in Ephesians.

God is indeed sovereign in the matter of grace. It is inconceivable that salvation should in any way depend on the individual, since it is part of God's overall plan as explained in chapter 1 and further developed in the latter part of this chapter and in chapter 3. Therefore verse 10 is an appropriate conclusion to this section, beginning with the words *we are God's workmanship.* The word *workmanship (poiēma)* was used in ancient Greek literature to refer to what a person made or did. Among other things it could refer to literary works, such as a poem. Christians used it in its more general sense and applied it to God's creation, as Paul did in Romans 1:20. Here, as the work that God produces, it stands in contrast to the mere human *works* in the previous verse that are unable to save us. Salvation cannot be our work, not only because it is God's work but because *we* are God's work, his new creation (2 Cor 5:17).

In fact, the word *created* is the very next word in verse 10. The sphere of God's creative activity *(in Christ Jesus)* is, as Andrew Lincoln observes (1990:114), the same as that of the natural creation (compare Col 1:16). The explanation that we were created *to do* [*epi,* "for"] *good works* carries forward Paul's major theme of purpose. These works were *prepared in advance,* certainly before we were saved, possibly even before the creation of the world. The only other use of this verb (and one Greek verb expresses the whole phrase *prepared in advance*) is in Romans 9:23. There, in contrast to those who reject—and are rejected by—God and are destined for his wrath, believers have been "prepared in advance for glory."

Titus 3:5-8 contains similar thoughts to Ephesians: "he saved us, not because of righteous things we had done, but because of his mercy" (v.

---

you. But the pronoun is neuter, and does not *necessarily* refer to faith. Even so, it may refer generally to faith: 'the difference of gender is not fatal to such a view' (J.A. Robinson)" (Bruce 1984:289, quoting Robinson 1904:157). In fact Robinson had said further, "But the

5); "and I want you to stress these things, so that those who have trusted in God may be careful to devote themselves to doing what is good" (v. 8). But while Titus 3, like Ephesians 2, emphasizes the condition of people before and after salvation, Ephesians has the added perspective of God's advance planning of the believer's postconversion life. In this context the point is not that every event is predetermined, good and bad (however that may be understood from other texts), but that God has prepared the good works believers are to do. This can be understood either as ethical ways to be followed or as specific instances of obedience. We are saved not *by* but *for* good works, and we are saved not just for a beautiful heavenly destiny that God has prepared but for good works here, likewise prepared by God.

Ephesians 2:10 therefore beautifully recapitulates the idea of God's plan and purpose set forth in the earlier part of the letter. This finds expression even in the very last phrase *for us to do,* which in Greek begins with the word *hina,* meaning "in order that." This final aspect of purpose has the flavor of an exhortation, "in order that we should walk in them" (NRSV "to be our way of life"). We have a happy obligation: to fulfill God's intention in saving us.

☐ Step Two in the Fulfillment of God's Plan: Reconciliation of Jew and Gentile Through the Cross (2:11-22)

Feelings of loneliness or alienation from others can be devastating. During the 1960s and 1970s many people expressed a deep sense of alienation. Philosophical, political and religious writers attempted to address the problem. Spiritually, those without Christ *are* alienated from God and from believers. I recall talking with a young woman at an InterVarsity student conference shortly after she had trusted in the Lord Jesus Christ as her Savior. She said that up to that point her feeling at the conference had been as though she was standing outside the building looking through a window at the Christians inside. She had been warmly received by the Christian students, but spiritually she had been on the "outside."

---

context demands the wider reference," and went on to say that the subject is "salvation by grace." Bruce himself in his conclusion took that "wider reference."

The social aspect of alienation appears frequently in the Old Testament. The people of Israel were instructed to show kindness to aliens who resided with them. One reason was that the Israelites themselves had been aliens in Egypt and should understand how they felt (Lev 19:33-34). Psalm 68:6 tells of God's concern for those who are without family or homeland.

Sometimes alienation takes the form of hostility. Tensions between Jews and Gentiles over the centuries, erupting tragically in Nazi Germany, are rooted in early history. In the time of the New Testament the Jews had reasons to dislike Gentiles. Devout Jewish people rightly deplored paganism, which often spawned gross immorality. While Gentiles could attend Jewish synagogues, and often did, even those who converted to Judaism had to do so on Jewish terms. The Jews naturally considered themselves near to God, while the Gentiles were distant. Paul responds to this understandable feeling in the section of Ephesians before us.

The kind of alienation described in Ephesians is even more serious than social disenfranchisement and hostility. It is a spiritual separation from God, of which social alienation is only one expression. Spiritual separation was defined in the first part of this chapter as being "dead." Social separation resulted in the estrangement and isolation of all Gentiles not only from the Jews but also from their God.

Paul skillfully points up this state of alienation by the use of graphic opposing terms of distance and proximity. The Gentiles, according to this section, "were separate from Christ, excluded from citizenship in Israel and foreigners to the covenants of the promise, without hope and without God in the world, . . . far away," separated by a "dividing wall of hostility, . . . foreigners and aliens." Through Christ believing Gentiles and Jews are now "near, . . . one new man [humanity], . . . one body," are at "peace," both reconciled to God, both having "access . . . by one Spirit" to the Father, both now "fellow citizens with God's people and members of God's household." Furthermore, Jewish and Gentile believers together constitute a structure that is "joined together . . . being built together to become a dwelling in which God lives by his Spirit."

This dramatic change took place through the death of Christ, who not only made peace (v. 15) but "is our peace" (v. 14). The transition in time before and after the cross is also marked by Paul by the use of contrasting terms: "formerly," "at that time," used with past tenses, and "but now," "no longer," used with the present tense.

The set of contrasts brings structure and vividness to the passage. It helps us to see the greatness of God's work and the qualifications of Christ to be head over all things through whom God will bring all things in heaven and on earth together (1:10, 22).

The Need for Reconciliation (2:11-12) The call to *remember* is intended to heighten the readers' appreciation of their present state of reconciliation. Jesus had said, "Salvation is from the Jews" (Jn 4:22). Paul wrote, "Theirs is the adoption as sons . . . the divine glory, the covenants, the receiving of the law . . . and the promises" (Rom 9:4). Gentile unbelievers, on the other hand, were two steps away from salvation: not only did they lack the blessings "in Christ" described in chapter 1, but they also stood outside of the context (Judaism) in which Christ had brought salvation. This passage teaches not that Gentiles should come to Christ by way of Judaism and circumcision, but that they had to be reconciled to Christ along with believing Jews.

Reference to the rite of *circumcision* (v. 11) was a blunt way of distinguishing between Jews and Gentiles. Elsewhere (Phil 3) Paul writes disparagingly of those who depended on their circumcision for salvation. The contrast in that case was between external and spiritual "circumcision" (compare Col 2:11). Here the contrast is between those who were in a covenant relationship with God and those who were not. It could be compared with the modern practice of excluding people on the basis of ethnic characteristics, but it goes beyond that, because to the Jews the lack of the physical mark of circumcision signified spiritual lostness.

The Way of Reconciliation (2:13-18) Paul describes the state of the Gentiles as hopeless, but this did not prevent him from seeking to build bridges with them as he did at Athens: "What you worship as something unknown I am going to proclaim to you. . . . He is not far from each one of us" (Acts 17:23, 27).

Jesus' Blood Is an Instrument of Reconciliation (2:13) The transition from "formerly" to *now* and from *far* to *near* is accomplished *through the blood of Christ.* This function of the blood of Christ may have seemed strange at first to a reader of this letter, and may seem even stranger to a new reader today. Yet not only is blood a way of designating the sacrificial death of Christ, but it also is seen in Scripture as a means of accomplishing various aspects of the saving work of Christ. We are reconciled by his blood (Col 1:20); it "purifies us from all sin" (1 Jn 1:7); we have been bought, acquired or redeemed through his blood (Acts 20:28; Eph 1:7; 1 Pet 1-18-19; Rev 5:9); and those whom Satan accuses overcome him "by the blood of the Lamb and by the word of their testimony" (Rev 12:11).

While some of the gospel hymns of the past hundred years or so may seem overly vivid in their references to the blood of Jesus, neglect of its significance would evacuate the gospel message of a central aspect of the saving work of Christ. It will help the modern reader to think of the blood as symbolizing the death of Christ or of his life poured out in death, but merely to substitute the term "death" in its place would be to lose the graphic intensity of the cross.

Jesus Himself Is Our Peace, Removing the Dividing Effect of the Law (2:14-15) We might have expected to read of *peace* as an objective that Jesus accomplished, as in verse 15, *thus making peace,* or as the content of the gospel, as in verse 17, *he preached peace.* But here it is a description of Christ himself, somewhat similar to the familiar "God is love" (1 Jn 4:8, 16). The next statement shows that this vivid concept that Jesus embodies peace is no mere rhetoric: unity between believing Jews and Gentiles was achieved *in his flesh* (v. 15). This is a reference to the incarnation and death of Christ. God "prepared" a body for him

---

2:14 For uses analogous to Christ as *our peace,* see 1 Corinthians 1:30, where Christ "has become for us wisdom from God—that is, our righteousness, holiness and redemption"; Colossians 3:4, "Christ, who is your life"; and 1 Timothy 1:1, "Christ Jesus our hope."

2:15 Opinions of biblical scholars on the role of the Old Testament law in the Christian era, as described in such New Testament writings as the Gospels and Paul's epistles, differ considerably. For example, when Jesus set his teachings over against specific commandments (as in Mt 5:21-30), was he annulling the latter, or was he perhaps intensifying them or drawing out their inner meaning? And how does one interpret Paul's comments about the law being brought to an end (Rom 10:4) and about "dying through the law to the law"?

(Heb 10:5), and therefore Jesus could bear our sins "in his body on the tree [that is, the cross]" (1 Pet 2:24). *To create in himself one new man out of the two* (v. 15) shows that Christ is the locus of God's work producing the new humanity. Compare *in Christ Jesus* (v. 13) with *in this one body* (v. 16).

When Christ *made the two one* (v. 14) he did more than introduce Gentiles to an existing body of Jewish believers. They were more than proselytes to a Jewish Christianity. The Jews had long anticipated Gentiles' coming to the Messiah, as passages such as Isaiah 11:10 and 42:6 and various rabbinical texts indicate. But this was different. This was a "third race," as it has been called, neither Jew nor Gentile but Christian. This passage even goes beyond that, for the word "race" implies a collective idea, a group, whereas the word *one* is corporate, a group described as an individual person.

The last part of verse 14 and beginning of verse 15 are difficult to analyze and interpret. The sequence of thought is basically that God has destroyed a barrier, removed hostility and abolished the law. The way Paul expresses each of these three actions raises some questions.

First, what did Paul have in mind when he wrote of a *barrier* being destroyed? Apart from some postulated cosmic barrier, or an ideological one, the probable referent is an actual partition in the Jerusalem temple area that excluded Gentiles from an inner court. An ancient sign forbidding Gentiles from going beyond the point at which it was posted was discovered by archaeologists in 1871 and has often been cited in this regard. But even more relevant is Paul's own experience of being arrested on the supposition that he had brought a Gentile into the forbidden area (Acts 21:27-29). Although his readers in faraway Ephesus would not be likely to understand this allusion, Paul would have had a

---

The positive comments by Jesus about the endurance of the law (Mt 5:17-20) and by Paul about its goodness (Rom 7:12) make it unlikely that the passage here should be understood to mean that the law was totally abolished. At the same time it should no longer be a factor in alienating Gentiles.

The Greek word for "abolish" is *katargeō*. It occurs also in Luke 13:7; Romans 3:3, 31; 4:14; 6:6; 7:2, 6; 1 Corinthians 1:28; 2:6; 6:13; 13:8 (twice), 10, 11; 15:24, 26; 2 Corinthians 3:7, 11. Bauer (1979:417) offers several categories of meaning. For recent discussions regarding the law in Pauline theology and in first-century Judaism see Strickland 1993, Thielmann 1995 and the discussion following comments on Romans 3:9-20 in Moo 1996.

vivid memory of this incident, which resulted in his trials and journey to Rome for legal appeal. Even if it was an ideological barrier, such as the dividing effect of Jewish laws, that was foremost in his mind, it is very likely that this disconcerting and crucial event lingered in his mind and feelings.

Second, what did Paul intend to describe with the word *hostility?* Analysis of the syntax can yield two possibilities, something like an optical illusion viewed from two different angles. Was he referring (a) to the *barrier* to which he had just alluded or (b) to the *law* mentioned in the next phrase? Syntactically *of hostility* could be understood as standing in apposition to either, but the sentence runs more smoothly if it is connected with the latter.

Third, is Paul viewing God's *law* as something hostile? It is because of a desire to avoid such an implication that some prefer to link the term *hostility* with the *barrier.* Some also suggest that it is not God's law in itself that is in view, but its extension and application *(with its commandments and regulations).* Paul's focus may be on the traditional derivatives of the law, which constituted a "fence" to prevent transgression of the law itself—a fence that also tended to exclude Gentiles. Some cite the food laws in particular, for Jews and Gentiles would not have been able to eat meals together.

During a study tour in Israel that my wife and I led, we had opportunity to feel something of what the Gentiles did in Paul's day. A few members of the group went ahead of the rest of us into the dining room of a hostel where we were to pass the night. They inadvertently sat in the wrong area and, just as they were about to pick up the utensils and eat, were suddenly warned to sit elsewhere. When we learned the circumstances we understood, yet as foreigners and non-Jews we felt excluded. No doubt Gentiles in Paul's day felt similarly excluded and perhaps did not understand why. We do know that the so-called fence around the law, the derivative laws that could keep a person from even coming close to breaking the biblical laws, both restricted Jews and restrained Gentiles to the point of exclusion of the latter.

The translation *abolishing* may suggest connotations that are too strong to apply to God's law. "Nullifying" might be better. The best paraphrase would be "rendering inoperative." The Greek word here is used with this general meaning in virtually every one of its New Testament occurrences. In Luke 13:7, for example, a barren fig tree "uses up" or "wastes" (NRSV) the soil; in Romans 7:2 a widow is "released" or "discharged" (NRSV) from the law of marriage. Understood in this way it can refer to the law itself, not just to applications that by their inconvenience alienate Gentiles.

If we note that *hostility* enters again at the end of verse 16, where Paul says it is *put to death,* we see that stronger language is used of *hostility* and the *barrier* than of the *law* itself. It is the effect of the law that is destroyed, and so in that sense the law itself as a force separating Jews and Gentiles has been rendered inoperative.

The Cross Has Brought a New Unity (2:15-16) With the separation gone, Jewish and Gentile believers have been brought into a new kind of relationship. Paul describes this unity as a *new man* (v. 15). This is a creative act: something exists that did not exist before (compare 2 Cor 5:17; Gal 6:15). It is not only that two formerly hostile groups have been reconciled to each other (and to God) but that together they form a new entity. *Man* is a translation of the gender-neutral *anthrōpos* in Greek (NRSV "humanity" is better).

It is difficult to know whether *in this one body* (v. 16) is another term referring to this new unity or whether it refers to the physical body of Christ on the cross. To be sure, Paul specifically mentions *the cross* in the same clause. But it can be argued that when Paul clearly has the crucifixion in mind in this passage he uses specific terms such as *blood* and *flesh* (vv. 13, 15). It is also true that in Ephesians, as elsewhere, Paul uses *body* as a term for the church (1:23; 4:4; and elsewhere). The cross may be in view in another phrase, *by which* or "through it" (NRSV), but the NRSV margin "in him[self]" reflects another possibility, that it refers to Christ rather than to the cross. Such uncertainties are not troublesome, since the passage as a whole makes it abundantly clear that reconciliation comes through Christ *and* through his death.

Jews and Gentiles Have Open Access to the Father (2:17-18) The ultimate goal of reconciliation is *access* to God the Father. The term for *access* occurs also in 3:12, a prayer where Paul relates it to boldness, confidence and faith in Christ. In Romans 5:2 Paul also links access with faith, in association with justification and peace. To come openly to God is in strong contrast to the previous situation of the Gentiles, when they were *far away.*

The Result of Reconciliation (2:19-22) Feelings of alienation or rejection may not have affected Gentiles in Paul's day as they might non-Christians today. Probably few Gentiles brooded over not having the same God as the small race known as Jews. But today there are a number of people who feel rejected by Christians where social or ethnic groups of the latter are dominant. Specifically, Caucasian Christians have established a reputation for displaying a low level of acceptance of others. Even the ideals cherished by many Christians of different races in the 1960s faded in subsequent decades, with many in despair turning to national pride and homogeneous churches rather than seeking to develop integrated relationships. While this is understandable from the social aspect, there is a spiritual unity that Ephesians indicates ought to be increasingly experienced by all believers. Paul describes this unity with graphic illustrations drawn from social and material structures.

The strong opening grammatical link, *consequently,* indicates that the subsequent circumstance is not merely desirable but a necessary result of the reconciliation of Jew and Gentile in Christ. The contrast between "then" and "now" is recalled by the words *no longer,* and *foreigners and aliens* alludes back to the "near" and "far" polarity. The social structures that now picture believers are (1) a mutual citizenship as *God's people* (literally, "saints") and (2) a family relationship with other believers *(members of the household of God).* Paul uses a play on words in which the word for foreigner *(paroikoi)* is contrasted with *oikeioi,* "household members." The same word occurs in 1 Timothy 5:8 in a literal sense, meaning one's own family, and in Galatians 6:10, meaning the family of believers. The *oik-* stem in these words is found also in the word for *building* in verse 21 and for both *built* and *dwelling* in verse 22. Therefore there is a lexical continuity in these illustrations.

The image of a family or household thus turns into that of a building, and then the building becomes a temple, somewhat like the "morphing" of a computer-generated picture. Paul proceeds to enlarge on his

---

2:20 The pursuit of the meaning of *cornerstone* will continue among the exegetes. See

imagery, specifying the foundation and cornerstone. Apostles here probably refers to the initial group of Jesus' disciples, possibly with Paul added, though others were subsequently thought of as apostles in a secondary way. The prophets are most likely those in the early church, rather than their predecessors in Old Testament times. That assumption is supported by the wording in 3:5 and 4:11, where both groups reappear.

But does *foundation of the apostles and prophets* mean the foundation consisting of those groups or the foundation that they laid? Since 1 Corinthians 3:10-11 says that Paul laid the foundation of Christ and others cannot substitute any other foundation, it is likely that the preaching about Christ is intended. A review of Matthew 16:18 may be helpful. The familiar "You are Peter, and on this rock I will build my church" may mean not that the rock is Peter the person but that it is Peter *confessing* Jesus as "the Christ, the Son of the living God." In this case Christ, whom Peter is confessing, is the important one, not Peter himself, and Christ becomes the foundation of the church as he is thus confessed. If so, Christ continues to be the foundation of the church as Paul and the other apostles and prophets preach him. So here in Ephesians 2:20, if the church is built on the foundation that the apostles and prophets had, it is their preaching of Christ (the apostles' preaching parallel to Peter's confessing) that constituted the foundation.

Whatever view is correct, the process of choosing one of these meanings must be coordinated with the interpretation of the description of Christ as the *cornerstone*. An immense amount of discussion has revolved around the meaning of *cornerstone* here. The basic problem is that the Greek word has different meanings in different contexts and can refer either to a foundation stone or to a prominent keystone or capstone. If it is the foundation stone, it would be a large stone at the bottom of the building, which, if laid accurately at a corner, provides a basis for aligning the other stones. If it is the keystone, it would be at the top of the building; its importance would lie in its prominence and possibly, depending on the construction plan, in its function of holding the other stones together, like the keystone in an arch. If the author had

the thoughtful remarks by Leon Morris (1994:78-79). For a concise but thorough discussion of *akrogōniaios*, see Lincoln 1990:154-56.

in mind Isaiah 28:16 (where the word appears in the Septuagint, the Greek translation of the Hebrew), it is a foundation stone. Isaiah's description of a "precious cornerstone," cited in 1 Peter 2:6, goes on to specify that it is "for a sure foundation." In 1 Corinthians 3 Paul says that he laid a foundation, which is Christ. Leon Morris has suggested that since the church is still growing, a stone for the top could not yet be in place, and that since Christ is already the cornerstone, this must refer to what is already laid—that is, the foundation (Morris 1994:79). That makes good sense, though the Ephesians picture of Christ as the head of the body and the goal of its growth may indicate that the prominence of Christ is the goal of the growing church, and this would fit with the keystone idea. (Since there is an element of imagery here, such logical maneuvering may be possible.) If my interpretation of the *foundation of the apostles and prophets* is correct, in that sense Christ is already the foundation as the object of their preaching, while in this part of the image he could also be the prominent capstone.

The idea of such a stone first appears in Jesus' teaching. "Jesus said to them, 'Have you never read in the Scriptures: "The stone the builders rejected has become the capstone; the Lord has done this, and it is marvelous in our eyes"?' " (Mt 21:42; compare Mk 12:10; Lk 20:17). Peter repeats this quote in Acts 4:11 and in his own letter, 1 Peter 2:6-7. Discussions of the image include Romans 9:32-33 and a group of verses in 1 Peter 2:4-8 surrounding the one just mentioned. Evidently the early Christians understood several "stone" passages in the Old Testament to be of great importance. Jesus may have given further insight on this as he taught his disciples during the period between his resurrection and ascension.

Robert G. Bratcher and Eugene A. Nida make a good observation regarding Jesus as the *cornerstone:* "Whatever the precise meaning of the word in Greek, the general meaning is not in doubt: Christ is called the most important stone in the building, the one that provides cohesion and support for the whole structure" (1982:63). While exegetes need to pursue the "precise meaning," preachers need to be sure that the truth of the "most important stone in the building" is not obscured in the process.

The function of a temple is to be a *dwelling* for God (though with the biblical understanding that God cannot be localized or confined to a building). So the previously alienated and sinful groups have now been *joined together,* stone by stone, so to speak, as a holy temple for the God to whom they have together been reconciled. It is striking that the words for *joined together* and *rises* (literally "grows") occur also in 4:15-16, where they describe the growth not of an inanimate temple but of the church as the living "body" of Christ.

God's "dwelling" with his people is a wonderful reality that began in Old Testament times. Paul taught in 1 Corinthians that believers, both together and individually, are God's temple, and that God dwells in each by his Spirit. "Don't you know that you yourselves are God's temple and that God's Spirit lives in you?" (1 Cor 3:16). "Do you not know that your body is a temple of the Holy Spirit, who is in you, whom you have received from God?" (1 Cor 6:19). That truth is repeated here, now with the additional emphasis on those who constitute what we might call the building materials.

☐ Step Three in the Fulfillment of God's Plan: God's Intention for the Church (3:1-21)

Some of us spend a good deal of energy rationalizing our behavior, covering up our real intentions (or spontaneity) and in general trying to appear as though what we do is consistent with deep-seated, well-thought-out principles. Paul wants to make it clear to his readers that far from such impromptu behavior on God's part, the inclusion of Gentiles along with Jews in the church was a consistent fulfillment of God's ages-old intentions. It was not some accommodation to circumstances. Paul wants his readers to seek an understanding of what God, in his infinite love and power, has been planning—even beyond all human comprehension. This will be his specific prayer in verses 14-21. He is about to express that prayer, introducing it with the words *For this reason I . . .* (v. 1), but he interrupts himself in order to establish a further point: God is working according to a plan that he began to reveal centuries ago and is only now working out.

God's Intention Is an Unfolding Mystery (3:1-6) Before Paul interrupts himself in order to give the background of the *mystery,* he mentions his imprisonment *for the sake of you Gentiles*. This demonstrates that he does not merely have a theoretical interest in their participation in God's *grace;* he is willing to go to prison to bring that grace to them. But there may be more than that to his unexpected reference to his imprisonment: he may be expressing intensity and even a covert appeal for them to listen carefully to what he intends to pray for them.

Paul considers himself to have been specially commissioned by God to explain God's *mystery,* describing this commission as an *administration*. The same pair of terms occurs in Colossians 1:25-27. In that passage Paul describes himself as a servant according to the "commission" (the same Greek word translated *administration* here) God had given him "to present . . . the word of God . . . the mystery . . . " (This passage in Colossians may be where Paul had *already written briefly* [Eph 3:3] about the mystery.) In Ephesians 3:9 he writes of *the administration* (NRSV "plan") *of this mystery*. And in 1:9-10 "the mystery of his will" is "a plan [the same Greek word as *administration*] for the fullness of time" (NRSV). The comprehensive scope of the mystery is therefore under God's administration, but as Paul preaches God's grace he is administering that phase of the unfolding of the mystery.

The mystery is neither inscrutable nor obvious; it can be known, but only by *revelation* (3:3) *by the Spirit* (v. 5), and requiring special *insight* (v. 4). The term *revelation* is important to our understanding of the inspiration of Scripture. (See notes.) The terminology in verses 3-5 shows something of the process by which God communicates his truth. Not everything God reveals becomes Scripture, but in this case it has, by divine inspiration. Through *revelation* God conveys to humans that which they could not know otherwise. Reciprocally, the recipient is

---

3:1 Some people may find it troublesome that in a book inspired by the Holy Spirit there should seem to be a lapse of memory or a flaw in organization that would cause the writer to break off a train of thought and go to another subject. They may be helped by the reminder that, in God's wisdom, the human beings who wrote were allowed to use their own tools, so to speak, of vocabulary, grammar, writing style and range of knowledge. God expanded or corrected their knowledge by revelation, guided their writing and so worked by his Spirit that what they wrote was totally in accordance with what he intended to convey. To see such a shift of topic in the middle of a sentence is not a problem for inspiration but a testimony to the God who can blend human characteristics and divine inspiration with a result that is perfect.

For more on Paul's view of his imprisonment mentioned in 3:1, see the comments on

given *insight* to understand the revelation.

The unfolding takes place step by step. Paul does not seem to say here that it had not been known previously at all, but that it *was not made known . . . in other generations as it has now been revealed* (v. 5, but see comments on v. 9 below). The *apostles and prophets* mentioned in 2:20 reappear as the recipients of the mystery. It is through his *Spirit* that God communicates this revelation. Elsewhere Ephesians describes the work of the Spirit in 2:22, 5:18 and 6:18.

Verse 6 explains the content of the mystery. It is not possible without awkwardness to convey the force of the Greek adequately in English. There are three words, each beginning with a form of the same prefix *syn-*, which means "together": *synklēronoma (heirs together), syssōma (members together)* and *symmetocha (sharers together)*. Each of these has particular significance in explaining the new relationship between believing Jews and Gentiles.

Heirs together picks up the inheritance theme from 1:14, 18 (which will reappear in 5:5). This means that Gentile believers are also God's children and, like Israel, inherit God's blessings. Inheritance, especially of the land of Israel, was of great importance and marked the special relationship of the people to their God. To be an heir of God is now a privilege of all believers. Galatians 3:23-29 teaches that before Christ came, those who were under the law were subject to that law as their disciplinarian. But when faith came, the relationship changed to that of children of God, among whom there is no difference of race, status or sex. And all who belong to Christ are "Abraham's seed" and thus heirs of the promise God gave to him. Galatians had already established that this promise antedated the law, and therefore the promise and the

---

4:1.

3:3 See the note on 1:9-10 for the meaning and significance of *mystery* in Ephesians.

Regarding the meaning of *revelation,* this is the process by which God makes known what has not been previously disclosed. There are truths that can be known through "general revelation," such as God's "eternal power and divine nature," which are "understood from what has been made" (Rom 1:18-20). But God has given further revelation about himself and other truths in Scripture and in the person of the incarnate Son of God. This is "special revelation." It is in Scripture that, for example, God's acts in history are further understood. Inspiration is the means by which God produced Scripture and conveyed this revelation to us. Not only the writers but also the Word itself is inspired (literally "God breathed"; see 2 Tim 3:16).

inheritance depend not on the law but on God's grace received through faith. This may sound complex and irrelevant to the modern reader, but on the contrary, it lays the foundation for all who come to God, not on the basis of keeping the law but of faith in God and his promise, Gentiles as well as Jews. This means we are all God's heirs.

Romans 8:17 says that "if we are children, then we are heirs—heirs of God and co-heirs with Christ, if indeed we share in his sufferings in order that we may also share in his glory." Gentiles therefore have now come into a privileged relationship with God from which they were formerly excluded.

Being *members together of one body* was very important for the Gentiles. The function of believers as a body of which Christ is the head is so essential to an understanding of the church that it is unthinkable that any group of believers should not be part of it. But once again, the Gentiles were formerly so far from God and his people that such an intimate relationship as membership in that body was beyond possibility for them. Since Ephesians lays such emphasis on the body (it is the basis of 4:1-16), the question of participation in the body by Gentile believers could not be overlooked or unresolved. By using a single strong term *(syssōma)* into which is compacted the idea of being members together of the same body, Paul loudly affirms the total integration and equality of believing Gentiles with Jews.

To be *sharers together in the promise in Christ Jesus* is an extension of being "co-heirs." But now heirship is specifically *in Christ*. This reminds us that not only do Gentiles have a privilege they did not formerly enjoy, but Jews also, even though they had been "near" in comparison with the Gentiles, have with them a new privilege. The blessings Israel enjoyed were not yet *in Christ*. Those who were physically descended from Abraham needed to realize that this in itself did not qualify them to receive God's spiritual inheritance. This is clear from Romans 9. Earlier in Romans (4:13-16) it was established that inheritance comes from God's promise, received by faith (compare Gal 3:23-29, cited above). In Romans 9:8 Paul asserts that "it is not the natural

---

3:7 It is difficult to achieve balance regarding the significance of service as a *diakonos*. (This is apart from its use for deacons in 1 Tim 3:8-13.) The verbal form *diakoneō* does

children who are God's children, but it is the children of the promise who are regarded as Abraham's offspring." So Jew and Gentile share in the promise, on the basis not of ethnicity but of incorporation together *in Christ*.

The term *in Christ* and its equivalents have already been used some eighteen times in the first two chapters of Ephesians. The original readers would have been attuned to the expression by the time they heard this conclusion to the section on the uniting of Jew and Gentile, so the term would have a rich significance for them. But even that important term is not the concluding one in the original text. That final position is held by the simple term *through the gospel*. The NIV text moves it up in the sentence with the effect of implying that the gospel is the means of the uniting of Jew and Gentile. The NRSV and NKJV keep it in its final place, which may stress, without minimizing the other words, that we share in the promise through the gospel. Neither of these placements is inherently wrong; each has its advantages. The final position in English does give prominence to the concluding phrase, in this case either *through the gospel* or (NIV) *Christ Jesus*.

God's Intention Is Fulfilled Through Paul and the Church (3:7-13)

It is always interesting to watch the faces of people who are being honored. At the annual Celebration of the Performing Arts at the Kennedy Center, when the TV camera focuses on the honorees, they always seem to be trying not to look too proud, though they properly feel they have a right to be. Similarly, the apostle Paul is genuinely aware of the importance of his ministry but at the same time wants to affirm his dependence on God's grace. He rightly considers it appropriate to explain his role in communicating the mystery and the gospel.

The Ministry of Paul (3:7-9) The sequence of thought in this section is (1) Paul's role is that of a *servant,* (2) his ministry is by God's *grace* and *power,* (3) he is conscious of his shortcomings, being *less than the least,* (4) his mission is to represent the *mystery* to *everyone.*

The word for *servant* is *diakonos,* a term Paul frequently uses to

---

not imply holding a special position, but the noun does seem to indicate someone who has a particular role in the church. A particular problem surfaces in the case of Phoebe in

describe himself and his associates in carrying the gospel message (Rom 16:1; 1 Cor 3:5; 2 Cor 3:6; 6:4; Eph 6.21; Phil 1:1; Col 1:7, 23, 25; 4:7; 1 Tim 4:6). The term conveys the idea of responsibility. It is not an expression of privilege, as we might suppose by the use of the word "minister" here in the KJV and still in the NKJV. The antecedent to that word in Latin *(minister)* signified one who serves, such as a waiter. The fact that the term "servant-leader" has come into use today in ecclesiastical and even business circles shows that we are beginning to see both the humility and dignity of service.

So Paul uses the term as one of dignity, feeling the need to explain that this is only through God's grace and power. The significant element here is not just being a servant, but being a servant of the *gospel.* In trying to assure his readers that he was not presumptive in taking this important role, Paul uses a self-effacing expression in verse 8. It is a grammatical combination of a comparative and a superlative form, *less than the least.* At times Paul seems unnecessarily to resort to extremely modest expressions. First Timothy 1:15-16 is often quoted in this connection: "Here is a trustworthy saying that deserves full acceptance: Christ Jesus came into the world to save sinners—of whom I am the worst. But for that very reason I was shown mercy so that in me, the worst of sinners, Christ Jesus might display his unlimited patience as an example for those who would believe on him and receive eternal life."

These are not the only places where Paul denigrates himself, however. In 1 Corinthians 2:1-4 he says, "When I came to you, brothers, I did not come with eloquence or superior wisdom as I proclaimed to you the testimony about God. . . . I came to you in weakness and fear, and with much trembling. My message and my preaching were not with wise and persuasive words, but with a demonstration of the Spirit's power." It has been said that it is the most saintly people who are most conscious of sin and weakness. In Paul's day it was customary for orators

---

Romans 16:1, where the masculine diakonos is used for a woman. Paul did not say that she "served" but that she was a *diakonos.* The masculine form of *diakonos* is used of Phoebe because the feminine form did not yet exist. Therefore she had a significant role, which was defined by the term *prostatis* ("benefactor"). Certainly, then, Paul had a special role as a *diakonos,* but he fulfilled it as a servant.

3:8 Some who deny Pauline authorship of Ephesians and the Pastoral Epistles claim support from passages in which Paul speaks of himself with apparent depreciation. Such

to claim a low level of ability so that their eloquence would be more impressive. But Paul does not seem to be manipulating his readers in that way.

In verse 8 Paul reaffirms his call *to preach to the Gentiles.* This was God's expressed intention at his conversion (Acts 9:15; see also 22:21; 26:17); Paul turned to Gentiles when his Jewish audiences did not respond (Acts 13:46), reaffirmed his mission to Gentiles at the conclusion of Acts (28:28) and wrote about it in his epistles (Rom 15:16; Gal 1:16; 2:2, 7).

The content of Paul's preaching to the Gentiles was *the unsearchable riches of Christ* (v. 8), a remarkable expression. The only other occurrence of the adjective *unsearchable* is in Romans 11:33, "His paths [are] beyond tracing out" (NRSV "inscrutable"). But if one cannot ever track down the full extent of the wealth of Christ, if it is unfathomable and its depths cannot ever successfully be probed, how can one preach it?

First we need to identify what is meant by the wealth or *riches* of Christ. Obviously it is not the amassed fortune of a Near Eastern potentate. On the contrary, Paul wrote, "For you know the grace of our Lord Jesus Christ, that though he was rich, yet for your sakes he became poor, so that you through his poverty might become rich" (2 Cor 8:9). Paul uses this term for wealth figuratively several times. Here in Ephesians it refers to God's grace in 1:7 and 2:7. In 3:16 it is "his glorious riches" (literally, "the riches of his glory"), referring to the abundant resources of God to provide all the spiritual help that believers need. In contrast Philippians 4:19 couples this idea of God's "glorious riches in Christ Jesus" not to spiritual but to financial needs. But in Colossians 1:27 the riches are those of God's glorious mystery. It is striking that according to Colossians 2:2 Paul wants his readers to "have the full riches of complete understanding" to know "the mystery of God, namely, Christ."

---

passages do not sound like the Paul they think they know. But it would seem less likely that if another writer were claiming Paul's name to commend the letter to readers, he would employ such a description as *less than the least of all God's people.*

3:8-9 Subtle differences between Ephesians and Colossians such as those between this text and Colossians 2:2 are taken by many scholars to demonstrate that the two epistles were not written by the same author; others take the difference to be a variation in sentence structure with essentially the same meaning. See the introduction.

So we have come full circle. Paul uses this graphic picture of wealth in various ways, but in Ephesians and Colossians it applies to his concern that people understand the mystery. The wording varies slightly between the two epistles. In Colossians 2:2 it is a wealth of understanding about the mystery, which is Christ, whereas in Ephesians 3:8-9 it is an understanding of the wealth of Christ with regard to the mystery. Therefore, to return to the meaning of *unsearchable,* Paul does expect that although the wealth of Christ, and especially of the mystery, cannot be fully explored, people will gain a degree of understanding that is sufficient for faith and life. "*Incomparable* riches of his grace" in Ephesians 2:7 may show that *unsearchable riches* here emphasizes uniqueness rather than inaccessibility.

Verse 9 repeats and intensifies Paul's claim to be preaching something not previously known (compare v. 5 and Col 1:26, which have similar wording to v. 9). The reference to God as the one who *created all things* emphasizes his sovereignty in connection with the unfolding of his mystery.

The Role of the Church (3:10-13) In my youth I once had the privilege of singing in a choral group under the direction of the legendary Arturo Toscanini. I was only one in a large group (along with a mighty orchestra), doing a very small part in the concert. Yet my sense of awe and my desire to do that little part well for the maestro continue strong in my memory. The huge audience could not distinguish any individual voice, but together we gave them pleasure and added to the reputation of the great Toscanini.

This section of Ephesians tells us that the church is destined to demonstrate God's wisdom to a heavenly audience. We may think that our individual voices count for little, but together we display the wisdom of God, the great Conductor of the church.

Verse 10 in the Greek actually continues the sentence begun in verse 8, though the NIV begins a new sentence for the sake of English style. It carries forward the explanation of Paul's ministry with a statement of its purpose. In verse 11 (still the same sentence in the original) there is a further statement of intent, this time referring to God's *eternal purpose.* The importance of this statement cannot be overstated; it is central to the epistle. The opening blessing (1:3-14) repeatedly affirms, in various words and syntactical constructions, that God has specific intentions for believers and indeed for the universe (see comments above on that passage). Verses 11-12 of chapter 1 make the remarkable assertion that we have been "predestined according to the plan of him who works out everything in conformity with the purpose of his will, in order that we, who were the first to hope in Christ, might be for the praise of his glory." God's choice was made "before the creation of the world" (1:4) and is now, in 3:11, seen to be an *eternal purpose* that gives meaning to the church.

Over the years I have participated in many discussions on the purpose of the church. This question was especially popular during the period when secular business was emphasizing "management by objectives." Inevitably, during the listing of various goals of the church, such as evangelism, world mission, humanitarian aid and so forth, someone would mention worship. Sometimes this was absolutized as the church's only valid purpose; more often it was either taken for granted or made into a fuzzy synthesis of all other activities. In Ephesians, however, the church is not pictured as *doing* worship but as *being* the display of God's wisdom. This brings him glory, which is the goal of worship.

God's *wisdom* is *manifold* (so also NKJV; compare NRSV: "in its rich variety"). This is the only time in the New Testament that this word occurs. It is a compound word, including the word for "many" or "much" and a word with such meanings as "many-colored," "variegated" and "diversified." The latter word was used to describe Joseph's "richly ornamented" coat (Gen 37:3) in the Septuagint (the pre-Christian Greek translation of the Hebrew Old Testament). The immediate text does not say so, but the reader can infer from the context that it is the complete uniting of Jew and Gentile in one body that demonstrates God's wisdom. That wisdom was introduced in 1:7-8 in connection with God's act of redeeming us through the blood of Christ, forgiving us and lavishing his grace on us. So from the beginning his wisdom was connected with his saving grace and his eternal purpose.

This recalls Romans 11:33-36: "Oh, the depth of the riches of the wisdom and knowledge of God! How unsearchable his judgments, and his paths beyond tracing out! . . . For from him and through him and to him are all things. To him be the glory forever! Amen." The subject of the preceding context in Romans 9—11 is the status of the Jews and also of the Gentiles in God's plan. Romans and Ephesians share this insight and the resulting doxology. As noted above, Paul uses the word "unsearchable" both in Romans 11:33 and in Ephesians 3:8.

While a church (that is, a local church and its members) can glorify God in many ways, we must remember that ultimately it is what *God* has done both for and in the church universal that brings him glory for his unsearchable wisdom. In this regard being is more significant than doing. This is the calling of the church above all callings. This is why it is appropriate that Paul will instruct us to *live a life worthy of the calling you have received* (4:1).

There is a surprising dimension to Paul's description of the calling of the church in verse 10. Those who observe the display of God's wisdom in the church are not other human beings but *rulers and authorities in the heavenly realms*. This introduces again the cosmic dimension of Ephesians. We learned in 1:3 that we are blessed in the heavenly realms and in 1:21 that Christ ascended "far above all rule and authority, power and dominion, and every title that can be given." We are "seated" in the heavenly realms (2:6). Now, like a million laser beams illuminating the heavens, the church penetrates the realms beyond with the display of God's wisdom. The description of heavenly beings surpassed by the ascended Christ (1:21) is reduced here in 3:10 to just two, *rulers and authorities*. It may be that these represent all the unseen powers, good and evil, but the fact that in 6:10-18 the rulers and authorities mentioned are only evil must be taken into account. See also the commentary above on 1:21 regarding the widespread ancient understanding of such powers as evil and the significance of that for this letter.

As noted above, it is important to realize that the inclusion of Gentiles along with Jews in the church was not an afterthought. All that Paul has described so far is *according to [God's] eternal purpose*. But it is not an unending project. It has been *accomplished in Christ Jesus our Lord*.

The next statement may seem to be an anticlimax. We know that faith in Christ is important, but that this enables us to *approach God with freedom and confidence* does not seem all that important in comparison with the cosmic truths in which Paul has just been reveling. However, this *approach* to God parallels the "access" to God of 2:18, which is the climax of the section on the reconciliation of Jew and Gentile to God and to each other. The present verse recapitulates that and ties it in with the display of God's wisdom.

The chorus of a hymn (or gospel song) that was once quite popular began, "Oh that will be glory for me." I recall one rainy day at a meeting in a YMCA in Queens, New York, when someone requested that song, perhaps to relieve the depression of the weather. The song leader asked us to change the words to ". . . glory for *him*." I often remember his request when I am reading Ephesians. There is much in the first several chapters about God's grace, and we naturally appreciate and thank God for what he has done for us. But it is too easy to be preoccupied with our benefits and overlook what God's grace means to him. We are saved by grace because that is appropriate to God's nature and purposes, bringing him glory as it brings us salvation. We are alerted to that at the very beginning of the epistle by the words "to the praise of his glorious grace" (1:6).

The sequence of God's saving acts in chapters 2 and 3—individual salvation, reconciliation not only to God but to one another and, even beyond mutual reconciliation, the uniting of Jewish and Gentile believers in one body—all this brings glory to him. His undeserved grace, by which we have access to the Father, is part of God's great purpose that has now been accomplished in Christ. Our Lord deserves all the acknowledgment that the sentient beings of the universe can give him because of the mystery and the wisdom that conceived it.

With such a mission to accomplish—that is, to help others understand the mystery and its implications—Paul is willing to endure *sufferings* (v. 13). When the readers understand this and realize that his suffering brings them *glory,* they will not be *discouraged.*

Summation and Affirmation in Prayer (3:14-21) Having described his own ministry and the role of the church in fulfilling God's intentions, Paul is finally ready to offer the prayer he was about to begin in verse 1.

Christians often feel ambivalent about prayer. We know that God has invited and commanded us to pray, that the Lord Jesus taught it and practiced it and that there are clear promises of God's commitment to answer prayer properly offered. But there is a lingering feeling that if

God wants to do something he will go ahead and do it, with or without our prayers. Yet the plain fact that Paul proceeds to pray for God's sovereign work in the lives of believers even after such a majestic exposition of God's purposes and their accomplishment should make the importance of prayer obvious.

We tend to think of prayer more as a means of setting our requests before God than as the means by which God accomplishes his work. In this context Paul's requests, when granted, *allow* God (so to speak) to do all that is described in 3:10 and its context. (For a discussion of biblical, theological and practical issues concerning prayer, see Liefeld 1986.)

Paul *kneels* (v. 14), not a common posture for prayer in his day. Standing or lying prone was the custom. This may be a signal not only of deep reverence but also of emotional intensity. He addresses his prayer to *the Father*, as Jesus taught us to do (Jn 16:23-27). Paul uses a play on words between *patēr*, "father," and *patria*, "family." It is difficult to know whether it is *his whole family* (NIV) or "every family" (NRSV) and exactly what Paul is saying by this play on words. He cherishes God's fatherhood over all his children. This is important for the unity of the church (2:18), but 4:6 points to a broader sense of that fatherhood. Perhaps, then, Paul is still thinking of God as the one who "created all things" (v. 9) and associating fatherhood with this role of Creator. This would not abrogate the unique fatherhood of God over believers (compare Rom 8:15-17), some of whom are *in heaven* and some *on earth*. So it may refer to that family *(patria)*, that is, all believers, or the cosmic family (understanding *in heaven and on earth* in that sense). Either way, the reason there is a relationship called a *patria* is that there is a *patēr*, a Father, over all.

Paul's petitions are related but distinct. The first is for inner strength (v. 16). It is the *Spirit* who accomplishes this, which is consistent with the fact that God dwells in us "by his Spirit" (2:22). Paul tends to multiply words of power, as he does here with the verb *strengthen* and the instrumental use of the noun *power* (compare Col 1:29). The abundant source of this enabling is *his glorious riches* (see comments on 3:8). The term *inner being* in verse 16 stands in parallel with *your hearts* in the next verse. This parallel is accompanied by a correspondence between

Spirit in verse 16 and *Christ* in verse 17. Christ is represented in our lives by his Spirit. In the Gospel of John Jesus says he is going back to the Father and will send the Spirit from the Father (16:28; 15:26—a significant trinitarian reference). But at the same time he says that *he* will be coming back to them (Jn 14:28; 17:11, 13).

There is a further parallel with Ephesians 5:18 and Colossians 3:16, which are in similar contexts. In Ephesians the command is "Be filled with the Spirit"; in Colossians it is "Let the word of Christ dwell in you richly." When we are strengthened inwardly by the Spirit, Christ is dwelling in us, and when we are filled with the Spirit, the word of Christ is dwelling in us. We could also say, in reverse, that the way to be strengthened within by the Spirit is to give Christ his right place in our hearts, and that the way to be filled with the Spirit is to be submissive to the word of Christ. This does not imply that a Christian may not have Christ dwelling within. It is rather that the verb, which combines the usual verb for dwelling with an intensifying prefix, implies a settled residence, as though Christ is not only living in the believer but making himself thoroughly at home.

Throughout Scripture the *heart* includes not only the emotional aspect of the person but also the will and the intellect. It is the center of the personality. Integrity and commitment are matters of the heart. Romans 10:8-10 illustrates the importance of the heart: to be saved you must confess Jesus as Lord but also "believe in your heart that God raised him from the dead. . . . For it is with your heart that you believe." Here in 3:17 Christ dwells in the heart *through faith*. The common phrase "let Jesus come into your heart" does not have a precise biblical parallel, but it is certainly permitted by this verse. The words of our Lord about knocking at the heart's door for entrance (Rev 3:20), however, are said to those who are already believers but in need of repentance.

From here Paul goes on (vv. 17-19) to center on love. The transition is not immediately clear. There are several unusual elements in this section. (1) There is a mixed metaphor, *rooted and grounded*, referring to planting and building respectively. That mixture is not a problem, as the referents are understandable. (2) In Greek these words are participles, but they are not connected to the rest of the sentence grammatically although their semantic connection is clear. (3) The words *in love* occur between the clause about Christ dwelling in our hearts and the clause about being rooted and grounded. This placement creates some uncertainty. The phrase probably belongs to the second clause, but if so why does it occur at this place, before the participles ("in love rooted . . .")? And why speak of being *rooted and grounded* in love?

In Ephesians 1:4 the word "love" occurs in a comparable position, between "holy and blameless in his sight" and "he predestined us . . ." It probably belongs with the following clause there also. It may signal a particular appreciation for God's love that led the author to put it in a prominent place. Verse 17 in chapter 3 may be an unconscious repetition of this syntax. Love also marks a significant transition in 2:4: "But because of his great love for us . . ." Therefore it is appropriate for Paul to reintroduce love as he contemplates what he most wants to request from God for the believers. It may also be that he is using this as a transition from his celebration of the unity of Jew and Gentile in the church to his plea for Christians to keep that unity through love (4:2).

Two questions have puzzled readers of verse 18. One is why Paul refers to four, rather than the familiar three, dimensions. The other is what it is that these apply to. The author seems to assume the common two dimensions on the horizontal plane (with each axis as one dimension, without specifying right and left, front and back). But when he comes to the vertical plane he seems to distinguish up from down, thereby making four dimensions. This may seem strange to us (though after Einstein we have become used to a different kind of fourth dimension the ancients would not have known of: time), but in the ancient world there was speculation about dimensions. This ranged from a lewd comedy scene of Aristophanes in which Socrates probes both up and down for new ideas to more sophisticated explorations into the nature of the universe (on the latter see Lincoln 1990:210-11). It is possible to ascribe too much meaning to this expression, which may simply be a pleonasm, or expanded language. One example sometimes cited is found in the words of Zophar to Job: "Can you fathom the mysteries of God? Can you probe the limits of the Almighty? They are

---

3:18 On the four dimensions of love see Barth 1974a:395-97 and Lincoln 1990:207-13. Bruce warns against determining the meaning via specific analogies (for example, in Gnos-

higher than the heavens. . . . They are deeper than the depths of the grave. . . . Their measure is longer than the earth and wider than the sea" (Job 11:7-9).

Even assuming a legitimate pleonasm, we still need to address the question of what is described in this way. It is commonly thought that the object is God's love. The reason for this conclusion is obvious: the love of Christ occurs in the immediately preceding verse (v. 17), and the following verse (v. 19) refers to knowing the love of Christ. With this bracketing one would expect love to be the subject of the intervening verse as well. Natural as that transition seems, the author does not make the connection grammatically. The NIV takes the topic to be love and deals with the grammatical break by knitting the two verses together, first interpolating *love* into verse 18 and then inserting *this* before *love* in verse 19 with this result (additions underlined): (18) *to grasp [the dimensions of] the love of Christ,* (19) *and to know this love . . .*

An alternative possibility is that Paul has wisdom in mind, given the fact that he has just written in verse 10 about God's wisdom being demonstrated in the heavenly sphere, which could be thought of as one of these dimensions. In support of this is a reference in both the context of Job and that of Ephesians to the four dimensions following (more closely in Job than in Ephesians) a reference to God's wisdom (Job 11:6).

One could leave the matter fluid and think of it as enlarging on the general concept of the divine resources that extend beyond our human comprehension. Ephesians 3:8 spoke of the "unsearchable riches of Christ" (see comments and other references there), and in verse 19 Paul describes the love *that surpasses knowledge* (compare also "the peace of God, which transcends all understanding," in Phil 4:7). The point is not that God's love (or peace) cannot be understood at all; otherwise there would be no reason to try to preach it or pray to know it. Rather, we will never be able to exhaust that knowledge. Further, in verse 20 Paul will praise God, *who is able to do immeasurably more than all we ask or imagine.* It may be that as Paul is overwhelmed with the boundless immensity of *all* God does, his mind moves from wisdom (v. 10) to love

tic writings). He cites the magical papyri to show that "dimensional language is liable to be used for a variety of unconnected subjects" (Bruce 1984:327 n. 96).

(v. 17) as the foundation and ground of our spiritual existence, and so as he continues in the expansive mood of verse 10 his thought is not limited to wisdom but envelops love, which (going from the general to the specific) he does not particularize again until verse 19, with only a thin grammatical boundary intervening.

To *grasp* the truth that Paul describes in this four-dimensional way requires more than personal intellect or intuition. We need *power,* just as we needed God's enlightenment to understand the wonderful truths in 1:17-19, and we need to experience this *with all the saints.* It may seem spiritual to sit alone and probe the meaning of God's resources in meditation, but spiritual exercise alone is insufficient. We need the power of God and the fellowship of believers as we share insights and experiences of God's wisdom, love and fullness beyond human comprehension.

The purpose of knowing this love is *that you may be filled to the measure of all the fullness of God.* The NRSV and NKJV "filled with" and the NIV *filled to the measure of* are different ways of translating the Greek "filled to" (or "toward" or "into"), which express a goal. Ephesians 1:23 says that the church is "the fullness of him who fills everything in every way"; 4:13 speaks of "attaining to the whole measure of the fullness of Christ." These are not easy concepts to understand. Colossians 2:9-10 contributes to the meaning: "For in Christ all the fullness of the Deity lives in bodily form, and you have been given fullness in Christ, who is the head over every power and authority." Without blurring the distinctive meaning of each of these other statements in its context, it is probably legitimate to summarize them by saying that the full divine nature of God, present in Christ even when he was "in the form of a servant," is available for us to experience. We should desire to approach God as he is, even in his holiness, through Christ, seeking to become like him, insofar as this is possible for a human being.

This state, in one sense, is already true of us, in that we have been reconciled to God, have drawn near to him and now can experience the indwelling Christ through the Spirit who fills us. It continues in real time. But there is also a future experience toward which we press, just as Paul wanted "to attain to the resurrection from the dead" (Phil 3:11) even though he already had assurance of having been "raised . . . with

Christ" (Eph 2:6). He was "called . . . heavenward in Christ Jesus" (Phil 3:14) and kept pressing toward the goal. Peter also grasped the force of the promises and the already/not-yet nature of Christian experience: God "has given us his very great and precious promises, so that through them you may participate in the divine nature [remarkable thought] and escape the corruption in the world caused by evil desires" (2 Pet 1:4). So as we comprehend the love of Christ we move toward being *filled to the measure of all the fullness of God. Filled to* (or "toward") expresses dynamic movement. In the context this certainly pertains to the fullness of God's love, but it can also be applied to his power, his holiness, his mercy, his righteousness and all that characterizes God and the kingdom that is also our goal.

We are now ready to join Paul in the closing doxology (vv. 20-21). The term "doxology" is used to characterize praise (here in prose form) that contains specific affirmations or reasons to glorify God. In this case those affirmations are (1) the fact that he is omnipotent far beyond our comprehension *(able to do immeasurably more than all we ask or imagine)* and (2) the resource and exercise of that omnipotence *(according to his power that is at work within us).* Just as Paul writes earlier in Ephesians on the surpassing greatness of God's being and attributes, so we cannot fully know God's power. Paul is fond of superlatives and expresses such expansive thoughts three times in the latter part of this chapter. In the previous paragraph he writes of the love that surpasses knowledge, and at the end of this doxology he maximizes the duration of time by means of the phrase throughout all generations, for ever and ever. In verse 20 he also uses a compound adverb that means immeasurably more than. Superlatives are difficult to translate because they are often idiomatic and express something more than or different from what the etymology of the term might suggest. Nevertheless, perhaps the awkward literal rendering "superabundantly more than" serves to express the elements of the original term.

And just as Paul writes earlier not only of the fact of God's grace but also of its application to our lives, so in verse 21 he emphasizes that God's power does not simply hover, as it were, in space. The fact that it is *in Christ Jesus* that God will receive glory is wonderful, but at this stage of the letter it is not surprising. What is perhaps totally unexpected by the reader is the phrase *in the church*. The churchs placed in parallel with Christ as the means of bringing glory to God.

This astounding statement brings chapters 3 and 4 to a resounding climax. God has saved us by grace, has reconciled us to himself and to each other, has demonstrated his wisdom to the heavenly beings through the church, and now is to receive glory in the church and in Christ Jesus through all generations, for ever and ever! Amen.

□ Step Four in the Fulfillment of God's Plan: The Unity of the Church (4:1-6)

It has become a common custom at weddings for the couple to light a unity candle. Two candles stand at either side of this larger candle, sometimes lit just before the service by the couple's parents, symbolizing their individual family origins. Then at the end of the service the couple take the two smaller candles, light the unity candle and then extinguish the individual ones. This symbolizes their oneness in marriage. Several couples I have married recently have chosen not to blow out those individual candles because, though united in marriage, we still retain our individuality. It is a lifelong task to be sure that neither unity nor individuality prevails to the detriment of the other. "And the two will become one" (Eph 5:31).

Ephesians 4:1-16 takes up the emphasis on the unity of the church from the previous chapters and shows how to express this in mutual ministry and maturity. But unity is not achieved at the expense of individuality. So after the list of the marks of unity in verses 4-6 (such as *one body and one Spirit*) Paul emphasizes individuality in verse 7: *but to each one of us.*

The Appeal for a Life Worthy of Our Calling (4:1) Paul initiates his exhortation with a reference to his own imprisonment. He does this also in his appeal to Philemon on behalf of the slave Onesimus. After calling himself a prisoner at the beginning of that letter he does it again in verse

---

4:1 Paul wrote several of his letters while he was a prisoner. See the introduction for the circumstances behind the writing of Ephesians. If this was the Roman imprisonment described at the end of Acts, the circumstances for his arrest were the following: During his missionary travels among the Gentiles he had collected funds from them for the poor

9. (The NIV's "I appeal" in Philemon 9 translates the same Greek word as *I urge* here in Ephesians 4:1.) In Philemon Paul uses the word once immediately before and once immediately after he identifies himself as "an old man and now also a prisoner of Christ Jesus." It is clearly a means of persuasion in Philemon, possibly seeking respect, possibly sympathy. Here in Ephesians Paul has already made reference to his imprisonment at the beginning of chapter 3, when he was about to express his prayer for them. There it may also be a form of persuasion, perhaps covertly urging them to listen carefully to what he, the prisoner, is going to ask God on their behalf (so that they will be open to what he desires for them).

Worthy of . . . appears in other Pauline epistles. In several cases the phraseology is clearly relevant to the circumstances. In Philippians, where Paul is concerned about the way the gospel is preached (1:15-18), wanting Christians be united in heart as they witness (1:27-30), he says, "Conduct yourselves in a manner worthy of the gospel of Christ. Then, whether I come and see you or only hear about you in my absence, I will know that you stand firm in one spirit, contending as one man for the faith of the gospel" (1:27).

In Colossians, just before his affirmation of the supremacy of Christ, he asks them to "live a life worthy of the Lord" (1:10). In 1 Thessalonians 2 the background is Paul's need to distance himself from charlatan preachers (pagan as well as professing Christian) who pursued an itinerant "ministry" for financial gain. In the center of the section dealing with this, Paul calls on the recipients of the letter as witnesses to his integrity. Part of the evidence is that he urged them "to live lives worthy of God, who calls you into his kingdom" (1 Thess 2:12). So it is that in his appeal for unity here in Ephesians he urges the readers, *Live a life worthy of the calling you have received.* Like the other references just cited, the original has the adverb "worthily," not the adjective *worthy.* None of us is worthy, but we can live in a worthy manner, as the translations try to make clear. The word in the Greek sentence, after Paul's exhortation *I urge,* is *then* (or "therefore"). The *calling* to which

in Jerusalem. He went to the temple to fulfill a vow and was falsely accused of bringing a Gentile into the sacred area, resulting in his arrest and trials. In Ephesians 3:1 he writes that he was a prisoner "for the sake of you Gentiles."

this points most naturally denotes all he has been saying about God's magnificent plan in chapter 1 (especially 1:14 and the prayer in 1:18, "the hope to which he has called you") and the fulfillment of God's purpose to unite Jews and Gentiles in the church as described in chapters 2—3. The readers have a weighty obligation to live worthily of their calling, especially to fulfill the great purpose expressed in 3:10-11, 21.

Some years ago, before the contemporary awareness about cigarette smoke, a cynic observed a friend smoking one cigarette after another of a brand whose motto was "They satisfy." His question to the smoker was "How many does it take?" The smoker was living proof that the commercial was overstated. TV commercials naturally feature, as evidence of their products' value, people who have been strengthened, slimmed or made prosperous by the product. The before and after pictures in a hair restoration advertisement are graphic examples. But Christian churches and organizations often are their own worst advertisement because of their divisions and competition. Doctrine, instead of uniting us (vv. 4-6), tends to divide us. Jesus prayed that we might be one so that the world may believe that the Father had sent him and loved them (Jn 17:21, 22). His prayer was answered in a way his disciples would not have expected, through his death, as Paul has just described in Ephesians 2:11-22, and through the fulfillment of the mystery described in 3:5. This is a case of the need to "be what we are." Ephesians builds on that principle.

Further, if (a) Christ is to be the uniting force for the entire universe (1:10), and if (b) through his death Jews and Gentiles can be not only reconciled to God but united together (2:11—3:22), then it is important to him that the church demonstrate his qualifications for the former (a) by displaying, in visible, practical ways, his capacity to do the latter (b).

The Qualities Necessary for Unity (4:2-3) Every desired quality in verse 2 is important for good interpersonal relations. This is certainly the case with being *humble.* Although the ancient Greeks despised *hybris,* an overbearing attitude that displeased the gods, they did not value humility. It is often pointed out that Christian humility is not a groveling attitude. Rather, it is an attitude of modest self-evaluation that characterizes devout people in both Old and New Testaments. To be *gentle* and *patient* is also important. The old King James word "long-suffering," though possibly misleading, conveys well the element of duration—in holding back from reacting against people—that is inherent in the Greek word. The qualities in Galatians 5:22-23, known as the fruit of the Spirit, overlap with the qualities in this verse. *Bearing with* would be "putting up with" in today's idiom. This is not irksome, however; it is done *in love*. Some notable divisions within the church over the centuries might have been avoided by the exercise of these virtues. Not all doctrinal controversies have been purely objective; personal pride and stubbornness have made their contribution.

It is often observed that verse 3 does not tell us to *accomplish* unity; that has already been done by Christ. It is now necessary to *make every effort to keep* that unity. This is not easy and requires diligence, but the task is supported by *the Spirit* who produces unity and by the encompassing *bond of peace*.

The Doctrines Basic to Unity (4:4-6) These great truths provide together an immensely strong reason to maintain our unity. A great many interpersonal, church and denominational divisions could have been avoided if those who differed had openly faced one crucial question relating to these verses: Are the reasons for separating from each other greater than the reasons given here for maintaining our unity?

The oneness of the *body* has just been explained by Paul in chapters 2—3. There is only one *Spirit* of God who indwells all believers, and the very unity under discussion is that *of the Spirit* (v. 3). This combination of one body and one Spirit occurs in 1 Corinthians 12:12-13: "The body is a unit, though it is made up of many parts; and though all its parts are many, they form one body. So it is with Christ. For we were all baptized by one Spirit into one body—whether Jews or Greeks, slave or free—and we were all given the one Spirit to drink." The *one hope* in which we have been *called* refers back to verse 1, which alludes to 1:18, which, in turn, must refer to what had just been explained in 1:3-14, including "the redemption of those who are God's possession—to the praise of his glory" (1:14). Once again in Ephesians our hope is not just what *we* shall experience and enjoy, but the joy and praise that shall come to *Christ* through those he has redeemed.

One Lord, one faith, one baptism is a familiar phrase. The central fact of Jesus as the only *Lord* is key to Christianity. We may sometimes think of it as promoting exclusivism (there being no salvation by any other name, as Acts 4:12 states), but here it is promoting unity.

The central affirmation of the Old Testament was "Hear, O Israel: The LORD our God, the LORD is one" (Deut 6:4), affirmed by Jesus in Mark 12:29. The title Lord was spoken by devout Jews in place of the name of God. Early in the New Testament period the same title was applied to Jesus, not merely as a courteous appellation (like "sir") but as a designation of deity. Christians could therefore imply deity by calling Christ Kyrios, Lord. The phrase "Come, O Lord!" uses the Aramaic word for Lord within the Greek text of 1 Corinthians 16:22, showing that during Paul's early Christian experience, while he was still in Aramaic-speaking Palestine, he became accustomed to addressing Jesus as Lord.

Several other New Testament texts are extremely important to our understanding of Christ as Lord:

Yet for us there is but one God, the Father, . . . and there is but one Lord, Jesus Christ, through whom all things came and through whom we live. (1 Cor 8:6)

No one can say, "Jesus is Lord," except by the Holy Spirit. (1 Cor 12:3)

If you confess with your mouth, "Jesus is Lord," and believe in your heart that God raised him from the dead, you will be saved. (Rom 10:9)

If we live, we live to the Lord; and if we die, we die to the Lord. So, whether we live or die, we belong to the Lord. For this very reason, Christ died and returned to life so that he might be the Lord of both the dead and the living. (Rom-14:8-9)

Therefore God exalted him to the highest place

and gave him the name that is above every name,

that at the name of Jesus every knee should bow,

in heaven and on earth and under the earth,

and every tongue confess that Jesus Christ is Lord,

4:5 Water baptism is distinct from Spirit baptism, but both were experienced by new believers in the narrative of Acts (Bruce 1984:336-37 and n. 17).

to the glory of God the Father. (Phil 2:9-11)

In these verses the title Lord ascribed to Christ identifies him with the Lord God of the Old Testament (especially 1 Cor 8:6; 12:3).

In most New Testament contexts *faith* means trust, but it also came to apply to the whole body of essential doctrine, as in Jude 3: "I felt I had to write and urge you to contend for the faith that was once for all entrusted to the saints." In both senses a proper understanding of Christ is essential. The word appears again in connection with unity in Ephesians 4:13, where it is linked with "the knowledge of the Son of God" and with maturity. There is a logical continuity from faith in Christ to faith as doctrine. Obviously, since it is a point of unity, it excludes individualistic, eccentric beliefs.

One baptism does not refer to the mode of baptism. If it did, the variety of practices in the church today would seem to nullify this whole part of Ephesians. In the New Testament period, baptism was performed out of doors and was a visible sign that the individual being baptized was now identified as a Christian. It was the one public act that marked all Christians. There is much discussion over the theology of baptism, its relation to the baptism of the Spirit and so forth, but that does not affect the significance of baptism in this context.

The argument for unity now reaches its climax in the nature of God (v. 6). The threefold structure of the preceding elements (body, Spirit, calling; Lord, faith, baptism) is now employed to heighten the "oneness" of God: over all . . . through all . . . in all. He is transcendent, pervasive and immanent. Each of these words is significant. For example, the fact that God is over all rules out any thought that the words in all might teach pantheism (the idea that God is not an individual being but rather that everything is an aspect of God). The word all may specifically allude back to the fullness of the church with its combined elements of Jew and Gentile. However, 1 Corinthians 8:6, which affirms the truth of this verse, extends the scope further, with the words (applied both to God the Father and to Christ) "through whom all things came and through whom we live." Through all, then, would mean that God's activity

---

4:6 When devout Jews came to the sacred name, *Yahweh*, in reading the Scriptures, they said "Lord" *(Adonai)* instead to avoid any possible blasphemy. (English translations usually reserve "Lord" for *Adonai* and use "Lᴏʀᴅ" for *Yahweh*.)

permeates the church and the entire universe. Nothing takes place in isolation from him. The third phrase, in all, is harder for us to conceive as applying to the universe, since Ephesians teaches that this is notably true of the church. The great climax to chapter 2 is that Jewish and Gentile believers now form a temple that is "a dwelling place in which God lives" (2:22). Yet in another sense, even heaven and earth cannot contain God (1 Kings 8:27; 2 Chron 2:6; 6:18). It may be that while the word *all*, repeated three times in this statement, can apply to the whole universe, the specific referent Paul had in mind is the church. This would fit the focus on the church throughout Ephesians. The larger picture is certainly in view in Romans 11:36: "For from him and through him and to him are all things. To him be the glory forever! Amen."

☐ **Step Five in the Fulfillment of God's Plan: The Maturity of the Church, Accomplished Through God's Gifts (4:7-16)**
Those who seek to shepherd God's people know that our unity is difficult to maintain and that maturity is difficult to produce. We also know from 1 Corinthians that unity depends in large measure on maturity, and that the latter requires spirituality (1 Cor 3:1-4). People cannot be whipped into unity, but God can bring about spiritual maturity and hence unity through the spiritual leadership he gives to the church. Paul explains in this section that these gifts were given by Christ himself.

The Importance of Individuality (4:7) The way by which Christ, through his gifts, brings about unity and maturity is, remarkably, through individuality. So after stressing *one* Lord, *one* faith, and so on, Paul says, *But to each one of us* . . . This stands both as a contrast to verses 4-6 and as an introduction to the section on God's gifts to the church (vv. 7-16).

The transition is marked by a change to the first person. A preacher who is eager to exhort the congregation on to better things may tend to use the second-person imperative. At times this is certainly appropri-

---

4:8 As part of a process of paraphrasing Scripture that was going on during the centuries around the time of the New Testament (especially in the Jewish interpretive paraphrases known as targums), the form Paul uses is somewhat different from that in the ancient Hebrew text. Whereas the Hebrew (and Septuagint) had "*received* gifts among men," Ephesians and the *Targum on the Psalms* have "*gave* [or distributed] gifts among men." The action is the same: the victor takes plunder and distributes it among his companions and

ate, but often it is better to join the congregation with a first-person plural (for example, "*We* should love God," rather than "*You* should love God"). Paul does just that in verse 7 and in verses 13 *(until we all . . .)* through 16.

This is part of a larger pattern. Not only does Paul move from unity to individuality as a theme, he also moves grammatically from the descriptive third-person mode of verses 4-6 (which, in turn, was a change from the second-person plural imperative of vv. 1-3) to the first person: *of us* (v. 7), *we all* (v. 13) and *we* in verses 14 and 15. In verse 16 Paul employs the third person *(from him the whole body . . . grows)*. Then from 4:17 through 6:20 he reverts to a series of plural imperatives.

The result of this structure is that Paul's commands are rendered more congenial because of the supportive doctrinal descriptions and Paul's own partnership with his readers. But this is more than a rhetorical device. What Paul is saying to the believers truly does involve him. He is the recipient of God's gracious gifts (vv. 7-11), and he is conscious of his need to grow in his knowledge of the Lord (vv. 13-16).

The Old Testament Basis for Christ as the Giver of Gifts (4:8-10)
The New Testament writers frequently quoted verses, used terminology and alluded to ideas from Old Testament passages. There were conventions for doing this that need not concern us here. What is important is that Paul sees significance in Psalm 68:18 in connection with God's distribution of gifts among Christian believers. The imagery in that psalm is of other mountains looking in envy "at the mountain where God chooses to reign" (Ps 68:16). God comes from Mt. Sinai, where he had revealed himself, and ascends to Mt. Zion, where he will "dwell." The references to "chariots" in verse 17 and to "captives" in verse 18 suggest a scene of conquest in battle. But whereas in the psalm the emphasis is on God's receiving gifts from the captives, in Ephesians it is on his giving gifts to his own people.

There is probably a further significance in Psalm 68:18. Gary V. Smith

---

others. To distribute it assumes first receiving it; to receive it implies subsequent distribution. Both phases involve the exaltation of the victor. Paul builds on this twofold imagery as it is fulfilled in Christ, first the exaltation and second the distribution. As in many other places where English translations have *men*, the Greek has the gender-neutral term for human beings.

(1975:181-89) saw a connection between that verse and the Levites as a "gift." In Numbers 8:5-19 the Levites are set apart from the other Israelites, who lay their hands on them, and they are presented to the Lord. Numbers 18:6 says, "I myself have selected your fellow Levites from among the Israelites as a gift to you [that is, to Aaron the priest and his sons], dedicated to the LORD to do the work at the Tent of Meeting." The Levites were presented to the Lord, who gave them to the priests, and Psalm 68:18 is apparently an allusion to this. Perhaps we may carry the analogy further by observing that in Ephesians those God chooses to serve are given to the church, which now constitutes a royal priesthood (1 Pet 2:9). It is important to observe further that God both gives his grace to *each one* (Eph 4:7) and gives particular leaders to the church (4:11). The latter are for the equipping of the whole church for ministry (vv. 11-13). We may say, therefore, that whereas in the Old Testament a select group (the Levites) were God's gift to serve another select group (the priests), in the New Testament all those God has gifted are given to all those who are priests—that is, all believers.

The quotation of Psalm 68:18 in verse 8 both enlarges on Paul's statement about the gift of grace in verse 7 and reaffirms the ascension and triumph of Christ, so important in Ephesians (see 1:20-23 and the various references to "the heavenly realms"). The Old Testament text speaks of Yahweh's ascent; the text here refers to Christ's. In view of that exaltation, it was natural for the reader to apply the imagery of the psalm to Christ. Paul's contribution to New Testament Christology through his teaching about the descent and subsequent ascent of Christ (especially Phil 2:6-11, building on Jesus' own teaching in Jn 3:13; 6:62) is reflected in this passage (vv. 9-10). The emphasis is clearly on the ascent, rather than the descent, with an expansive phrase, *higher than all the heavens,* and the subsequent purpose clause, *in order to fill the whole universe.* The idea of filling the universe conforms to 1:23 and calls to mind the idea of the filling in other contexts: Ephesians 3:19; 5:18; and Colossians 1:9, 25; 2:10.

4:9 The wording used in the NIV, *lower, earthly regions,* interprets the Greek (literally, "the lower [parts] of the earth") as expressing apposition: the "lower parts" *are* the earth. The other grammatical possibility, that it is partitive—meaning the parts that are at the bottom of the earth, that is, the "underworld"—is understood by some to uphold the concept

The Nature of the Gifts (4:11) The very idea of receiving a gift excites most people, and so it is not surprising that in the Christian world some have taken great delight in investigating their own spiritual gifts. Yet when it comes to a serious consideration of what Scripture actually teaches and how one can become more involved in building the church through the use of these gifts, there is often disinterest and confusion. What must be kept in mind is that the gifts here in verse 11, those in Romans 12:3-8 and those in 1 Corinthians 12:1-31 are not for our personal benefit. They are given by God for the good of others ("to prepare God's people," v. 12; compare "for the common good," 1 Cor 12:7).

In Ephesians 4 the gifts named are not abilities given to people; they are people given to the church. It is not certain whether Paul puts any emphasis on the order in which he lists them here. In 1 Corinthians 12:28 the term "first of all" occurs before "apostles," with "prophets" named "second" and "teachers" "third." Earlier in Ephesians it is clear that the apostles and prophets had a foundational ministry (2:20). The prophets, being named after the apostles, are not Old Testament prophets but those active in the church. Both, therefore, are among the "gifts" in this passage.

Apostles were more than what we would call "church planters" today. The first people named apostles in the New Testament were limited in number to twelve, apparently representative of the twelve tribes of Israel. That could be the reason that after the death of Judas Iscariot they needed to maintain a membership of twelve (Acts 1:15-26). While it may be debated whether that number was extended to allow others to have the title *apostle* in the same sense as the Twelve, at least Barnabas and Paul were called such ("the apostles Barnabas and Paul," Acts 14:14). There were also "false apostles" (2 Cor 11:13; Rev 2:2). While there are those who do pioneering evangelism and church planting today, the use of the term *apostle* (beyond the Twelve) is so sparse in the New Testament that it may be better to refrain from applying it in anything

that Christ descended to hell after his death. The traditional wording of the Apostles' Creed, "he descended into hell," reflects that latter understanding, though in its history it did not always imply that. "Lower parts" here means earth itself.

but an informal way to church or missionary leaders today.

Prophets were very active in the early church. Acts mentions several specifically: the four daughters of Philip the evangelist (Acts 21:8-9) and Agabus (Acts 11:28; 21:9-11). In addition 1 Corinthians 11:1-16 pictures church meetings where men and women prophesied. Prophets could, but did not necessarily, predict the future. God spoke through them to people who needed specific direction or exhortation. They bring the living word of God to bear on a particular circumstance. Their mention here shows that their function was important and was more than a passing activity.

The term *evangelist* requires some rehabilitating in our day because of its common connotation of flamboyant TV preachers with a craving for money. In the New Testament evangelists conveyed the "good news" about Jesus Christ. This good news, the gospel, centered on the death, burial and resurrection of Christ, especially the fact that "Christ died for our sins according to the Scriptures" (see 1 Cor 15:1-8). Those who were gifted as evangelists did more than witness, which is expected of all Christians. Witnesses openly acknowledge their faith in Christ and testify to what Christ has done for them; evangelists declare the gospel seeking converts. Paul told Timothy to "do the work of an evangelist" (2 Tim 4:5). It is probable that evangelists extended the work of the apostles. Paul, for example, took the gospel to Ephesus; Timothy continued that ministry.

The inclusion of *evangelists* in Ephesians 4:11 makes the important point that the function of the evangelist is to help in the building of the church. We might say that the other gifts are for the edification of the church, whereas evangelism is for the augmentation of the church. God did not intend evangelism to be carried on without regard to the local church and its ministry. Paul and Barnabas's missionary journey was commissioned by the church at Antioch (Acts 13:1-3).

There has been some question as to the significance of the fact that in Greek the words *pastors* and *teachers* are joined by a single article rather than individualized with each having its own article. This device usually indicates that the words so joined stand in a close relationship; in some cases their meanings are identical. Are *pastors* and *teachers* two terms for the same people, then, or terms that show closely related functions of different people? Paul told the Ephesian elders to be "shepherds of the church of God" (Acts 20:28; compare 1 Pet 5:1-4). But though all elders seem to be pastors, only some are teachers (1 Tim 5:17). Pastors must feed their sheep (with the Word of God), and teachers should apply biblical truth to the pastoral needs of the flock. Thus the gifts are related, but some people will be better suited to teaching and some to shepherding.

It is especially interesting that Paul combines teaching and shepherding equally here when in his opinion teaching is of extraordinary importance (Rom 12:7; Col 3:16; 1 Tim 3:2; 4:11; 6:1; 2 Tim 2:24; Tit 2:1-3, 15). The importance of the teacher grew in the subapostolic church. After the apostles, who taught with authority the teachings of and about Christ, the church needed a more settled ministry of those who would repeat the traditions and then teach the Scriptures as they became available and accepted. Ultimately the use of the Greek term for teaching, *didachē*, lessened, and the word group from which our term "catechism" is derived came into common use. Teaching became the repetition of accepted truth; teachers were rarely itinerant.

Recently the issue of whether verse 11 describes functions or offices of ministry has received much attention. One reason this is a difficult issue to resolve is that some of the epistles emphasize function (notably 1 Cor) whereas others, specifically the Pastorals, are thought to embody the idea that only certain designated persons carry on the major ministries of the church. It has been said that the Corinthian atmosphere is charismatic, but not that of the Pastorals. The differences are not as marked as sometimes thought. First Corinthians 12:27-31 lists specific classes of people doing ministry, and conversely 1 Timothy speaks of "gift" and a "prophetic message" in the very passage that used to be (mistakenly) thought of as portraying ordination (4:14).

If pastors and teachers are to be thought of as offices, one has to demonstrate first that there were "offices" in the New Testament church. There is no Greek word in the New Testament corresponding to "office." The term did occur in the King James Version, but without warrant in the Greek text.

The Purpose for the Gifts (4:12-16) Verse 12 continues the sentence begun in the previous verse. It initiates a series of constructions each of which connotes purpose: "toward" or "for" (v. 12), *until* (v. 13) and "in order that" (*hina*, NIV's *Then,* v. 14). We are in the same mode of thinking as in 1:3-14, where the idea of purpose dominates much of the wording and grammatical structure.

The first of these constructions, "for the preparation/equipping of God's people" (literally "saints"; NIV *to prepare God's people*), is a prepositional phrase that occurs in conjunction with two other such phrases, literally, "for work that consists of service" (often translated "work of ministry") and "for [the] building up of the body of Christ." A major exegetical issue affects the interpretation of the successive phrases "for equipping," "for ministry," "for building up": are they (1) in parallel (that is, coordinate), (2) in sequence or (3) mixed?

If they are in parallel (1), the leaders do all three of the following: equip the people, do the works of service and build up the body. If they are in sequence (2), the gifted leaders equip the people, who in turn do the works of service, which in turn result in the building up of the body of Christ. If they are mixed (3), the leaders equip the people, who in turn actively do both of the following: the works of service and the building up of the body. In effect, options 2 and 3 are similar; only in 1 would the leaders be understood as doing all the ministry themselves. So there are two major alternatives: either the leaders do all three tasks (the phrases in parallel), or they prepare God's people and thus achieve the goals of service and building through the people themselves. While the grammar could support the idea that in this particular place Paul is focusing only on the ministry of the leaders, we know from verse 7 that every believer is gifted and contributes to the building up of the body. That is the most likely meaning here in verse 12.

However this issue is resolved, it is clear that the leaders have the responsibility of preparing others. The word *prepare* or "equip" (NRSV),

_____

4:12 The literature on gifts, function and office is vast. Bengt Holmberg (1980:109-21) summarizes much of the earlier discussion on function and office. One of his useful contributions from a sociological perspective is a discussion on what constitutes an "office." An excellent study of Ephesians 4, with both biblical and sociological insights, is White 1987. See also Fung 1980, Fung 1982, Banks 1988:91-121 and Best 1993.

4:12-13 Part of the resolution of the issue of whether the successive phases for equipping, ministry and building up are in parallel or in sequence depends on the function

while translated as a verb for smoothness in English, is a noun in Greek. It refers to a situation in which a person or thing is in need either of completion or of restoration. Perhaps the closest parallel in the New Testament is the occurrence of the verbal form in 1 Thessalonians 3:10, "Night and day we pray most earnestly that we may see you again and *supply* what is lacking in your faith." Here in Ephesians it is the outfitting of Christians for the works of service God has given them to do. We speak of people going to seminary to "prepare" for ministry. But today's students often have already been engaged in spiritual ministries and need only to become "complete." In Luke 6:40 Jesus speaks of a student's being "fully trained," a related adjective in the Greek that also means "complete." In 1 Corinthians 1:10 the word "complete" is used in the corporate sense ("no divisions among you . . . but complete"; NIV *perfectly united*), an emphasis that is compatible with the emphasis here on unity and maturity.

This training or equipping is for "ministry." *Service* is the most straightforward translation of the word Paul uses *(diakonia)*. Although it refers to such things as teaching the Scripture and missionary work (as in Acts 6:4; 12:25), in itself it does not have the ecclesiastical overtones it does today. Whatever is done for God and in his name for people is a ministry.

The image of building assumes a discernible point at which the building will be completed. A contractor has the architect's plans, which show when a building has reached its vertical and horizontal limits. But the building of a *body* requires a different measure. In physical "body building" the goals are relative: muscle size and tone. The building of an individual or a group of people spiritually, however, requires a still different means of assessment. Therefore in verse 13 Paul provides the proper yardstick: maturity, which is further defined as *the whole measure of the fullness of Christ*. This helps our understanding of a word that

---

of the prepositions. Does the difference between *pros* (which introduces what all agree is the work of the leaders—*prepare God's people*) and *eis* (used in the phrases *for works of service* and "for the building up . . .") separate the specific ministry of the leaders from that of all the people together? And does the repetition of *eis* link the works of service and building up of the body as both being the ministry of all the people rather than just of the leaders? Or is there no intended difference between *pros* and *eis*, in which case all three phrases *could* (but not necessarily) describe only the specific ministry of the leaders?

tends to be obscured in translations, *teleios,* which can mean perfect or complete. In verse 13 it modifies the word for "man," and the phrase could be translated a "perfect man," or a man who is complete. While "maturity" (NRSV) is a possible idiom to represent this, maturity can be a relative term, and we must not lose the sense of a definable goal toward which the church should press.

A good deal of research has gone into assessing what constitutes maturity in various areas of intellectual, social and spiritual life. *Knowledge* is usually considered a part of maturity, and that is reflected here in verses 13-14. But there is more to maturity than knowledge. One important aspect is the ability to relate well to others and to support one another. Verse 13 combines the ideas of maturity and knowledge with that of unity, already introduced in 2:11-22 and in 4:3-6. All this explains what it means for the body of Christ to be built up.

But these three terms, "maturity," *knowledge* and *unity,* are not abstract idealizations. Each has a specific referent. To take them in the order of verse 13, *unity* is *in the faith.* The definite article refers here to faith as a body of doctrine, not to faith as an act of trust (compare v. 5). Christians are not called to maintain unity with those who do not hold to *the* faith, which is, in all the New Testament and early church confessions, linked with the person and work of Christ. But we are called to transcend noncrucial differences (such as mode of baptism, kind of ministry, style of worship) for the sake of unity.

Likewise, the *knowledge* has a specific object: *the Son of God.* Ephesians refers to Christ in different terms, but this is the first time it uses this one, so familiar from other parts of the New Testament. Two reasons for its use here seem probable. One is that verse 14 will warn the readers about false teachers, and the divine sonship of Christ is always doctrinally crucial. Another is that this passage deals with future growth, and the full comprehension of the exalted Son of God is a goal to which Christians will always press.

4:14 Other examples of accusation of deceit occur in Matthew 27:63, where it is falsely used against Jesus; 2 John 7, where those who deny the truth about Jesus "have gone out into the world"; 2 Timothy 3:13, "while evil men and impostors will go from bad to worse, deceiving and being deceived"; and 1 Thessalonians 2:3-5, "For the appeal we make does not spring from error or impure motives, nor are we trying to trick you. On the contrary,

In 1:23 Paul wrote of the church, the body of Christ, as "the fullness of him who fills all in all" (compare Col 2:9-10). Apparently there is in Paul's mind an idea of the wholeness of the church that is our goal. Although we may take this goal as a measure of our own spiritual growth, and although it may remind us of the perfection of Christ himself, the goal is a corporate state. We can measure our own maturing progress by that measure. Individuality comes in when we realize that as long as any of us is a child, easily misled by false doctrine (v. 14), we do not "measure up," and that corporate goal is not yet reached.

We often grasp the meaning of an idea better when we are confronted with a contrast. Verse 14 provides just that, a picture of immature people who, in a change of metaphor, find themselves floundering in a sailing vessel, lurching back and forth, violently tossed about by wind and waves. (In Jude 13 apostates are "wild waves of the sea, foaming up their shame.") The metaphor changes again as the treacherous winds change from the content of false teaching to the methods: *cunning* trickery, *craftiness* and *scheming*.

The word for *infants* can mean minors or babies. It signifies the opposite of maturity. The three main terms that follow form an interesting sequence: (1) *cunning*, (2) *craftiness* and (3) *deceitful scheming*. The first denotes dice playing and thus connotes the clever ways a professional gambler tricks an opponent. The second signifies unscrupulous evildoing. Today we might use the metaphor of "dirty pool." Paul specifically rejected such activity in 2 Corinthians 4:2: "Rather, we have renounced secret and shameful ways; we do not use deception [or 'craftiness,' the word used here in Ephesians], nor do we distort the word of God. On the contrary, by setting forth the truth plainly we commend ourselves to every man's conscience in the sight of God." The third means scheming in a deceitful way. The word *scheming (methodeia)*, like our English word "manipulation," can have a positive or negative connotation, but the context indicates the latter. *Deceitful* may seem

---

we speak as men approved by God to be entrusted with the gospel. We are not trying to please men but God, who tests our hearts. You know we never used flattery, nor did we put on a mask to cover up greed—God is our witness." Itinerant preaching was an easy means for greedy, unscrupulous people to solicit money. The bad reputation some TV preachers have brought on themselves is the closest parallel today.

strong, but the charge of deceit is frequently found in the literature describing itinerant preachers who were one's rivals, both pagan and Christian, in the early Roman Empire. It was customary to hurl demeaning language at one's competitors, but Christians were especially concerned with truth and so often applied the word *planē*, which means *deceit* or *error*, to the heretics' methods and teachings. This is also the case within the New Testament (2 Pet 2:18; 3:17; 1 Jn 4:6; Jude 11).

Speaking the truth in love (v. 15) counters the elements of deceit and evil cited in verse 13 and returns to positive exhortations. The choice is between truth and error, between love and hostile intentions. Truth in Scripture implies dependability and integrity. This is God's nature, and Jesus, God in human flesh, was "full of grace and truth" (Jn 1:14). The words *grow up* (v. 15) are in contrast with *infants* in verse 14.

But now the image becomes that of a body and its head. Today we use the word *head* frequently to refer to the chief executive officer of a corporation, a nation's leader ("head of state") and similarly to other leadership positions (head nurse, head waiter and the like). This makes it difficult for us to understand that in ancient Greek literature there were other uses that were not connected with rule or authority. But in verses 15-16 the second of two prepositions used in connection with the imagery of the head is difficult to relate to headship as rulership. In verse 15 we *grow up into him,* and in verse 16 the growth of the body is *from [literally "out of"] him*. The latter idea accords with the unusual meaning of *head* as source. This idea of the head as source is hardly found in figurative language in Greek literature, but it is found in ancient medical literature. However the linguistic issue may be resolved, in this context the imagery seems clear, and it is rich: (1) Christ as Head is the source of growth, (2) the body grows *into* Christ, and (3) each part does its work. So the body responds to the head and its provision.

4:15-16 Much has been written on the topic of headship in recent years. It was long assumed that *head (kephalē)* always carried the connotation of "chief," "ruler" or authority, as it often does in English. This was the case with the Latin *caput,* which is reflected in the early church literature in that language. This began to be challenged seriously, and an example of the state of the discussion in the mid-1980s appears in Mickelsen 1986. An article by Wayne A. Grudem (1985), which concentrates on a group of figurative uses among the thousands of occurrences of the word, took the older view of authority. Gordon Fee sharply criticized it shortly afterward (1987:502-3 nn. 42-46). In that same year an argument

As Paul explains the functional unity of the body, he notes that each *ligament* provides connection to support the parts of the body as they work together. Ligaments are important, a fact now familiar from the number of sports injuries that plague both professionals and amateurs. The reference to "each part" emphasizes the truth of verse 7. Once again Paul uses the phrase *in love*. This gives a personal dimension to the physical description of body building.

☐ **Step Six in the Fulfillment of God's Plan: Christian Morality Accomplished Through a Radical Change (4:17—6:9)**
Of the three characteristics that Ephesians says should mark Christians, unity, maturity and morality, the third is the most overt and easy to distinguish. A major breach of unity is, of course, visible when it eventuates in a church split, but underlying attitudes between Christians are less easy to observe. Maturity by its nature is gradual; neither maturity nor immaturity is always apparent. Immorality, on the other hand, is often glaring, especially when expressed in gross acts and, sadly, when committed by those in leadership.

The Need for a Radical Change (4:17-19) Christians are often perplexed when their attempts to explain the truth of the gospel to others fail to be understood and accepted. There can be several reasons for this. One is simply Christians' lack of perceptiveness regarding what words and ideas are so new and different that there is a need for further explanation. Another is the direct opposition of Satan: "the god of this age has blinded the minds of unbelievers, so that they cannot see the light of the gospel of the glory of Christ, who is the image of God" (2 Cor 4:4). In between these is the hardened state of the heart and mind of an unbeliever that results from continued resistance to God. This may

appeared for the meaning "source" (Kroeger 1987). Following other discussions, Grudem (1991) summarized the matter from his viewpoint. In 1993 a further article by Kroeger brought her research up to date.

4:16 Ephesians contains an unusually high number of occurrences of the word *love*, especially considering the brevity of the epistle. *In love* occurs in 1:4; 3:17; 4:2, 15, 16; 5:2 (NIV translates "live a life of love"), and other uses of the word are in 2:4; 3:18, 19; 5:25, 28, 33; 6:23, 24 (twice).

include the direct work of Satan, but that is not stated here.

The vividness of Paul's descriptive terminology serves both to explicate his ideas and to elicit a response from the readers/hearers. There is an emotive content to words like *futility* (v. 17); *darkened, separated, ignorance, hardening* (v. 18); *sensitivity, sensuality, indulge* and *lust* (v. 19). When this is combined with the intellectual content of the words *thinking* and *understanding,* the total picture is clear. It also forms a contrast to "speaking the truth in love" (v. 15).

This paragraph also contrasts with the following one, which begins, "You, however . . ." (vv. 20-24). That paragraph, in turn, introduces 4:25—5:2, "Therefore each of you must put off . . ." Verses 19-24 here are similar to parts of Colossians 3:5-10. Within these passages the most obvious similarity is the idea of "putting off" the old self and putting on the new. The sense of inevitable downward progress here in Ephesians 4:17-19 also echoes parts of Romans 1:21-25: (1) futility of thinking, (2) darkening of understanding (Romans "hearts") and (3) being given over to impurity (in Romans, by God; in Ephesians, by themselves).

It may seem strange that Paul needs to urge Christians not to live this way. One would think that they would have been so glad to be free of their old life that it would not occur to them to retrogress. It may be, however, that some had returned to old practices without realizing the serious significance and implications of what they were doing. We do know that by the end of the century the church that bears the name of this epistle had forsaken its first love and needed to repent (Rev 2:4-5).

People need a sense of meaning and worth. That became clear through motivational studies many decades ago. *Futility* is a vacuum of accomplishment. The promise of meaningful purpose and fulfillment can be a powerful incentive to become a Christian believer. But this motivation is not effective among the Gentiles described here, because these very people are devoid of understanding and hard of heart. *The futility of their thinking* perhaps serves therefore as a stronger motivation to believers not to return to that way of life than to those who have not been converted.

4:19 The unresponsiveness Paul describes in this section seems similar to that mentioned in 1 Timothy 4:2: "whose consciences have been seared as with a hot iron." In that case, however, the individuals were not unconverted Gentiles but apostate Christians.

The *understanding* that is *darkened* (v. 18) is the *dianoia,* the mind. It is sometimes associated with the *heart.* We are to love God with our heart, soul and mind (Mt 22:37; compare Mk 12:30; Lk 10:27). Hebrews 10:16 quotes the following from Jeremiah 31:33: "I will put my laws in their hearts, and I will write them on their minds." The biblical use of *heart* is not mainly as the source of emotion, but as the center of the whole personality. *Mind* denotes *understanding,* but its meaning also overlaps with that of *heart.*

The reader of verse 18 may think that there is a touch of unfairness in people's being *separated from the life of God* because of *ignorance* and *darkened . . . understanding.* But to think this is to miss the sequence of the wording and the thrust of the passage. These Gentile unbelievers do not have the life of God *because of* (*dia,* "on account of") the *ignorance* that (in turn) is *due to* (again, *dia*) *the hardening of their hearts.* Therefore it is their own hardness against God that perpetuates their alienation from God's life.

Given this condition, there is a lack of *sensitivity* (v. 19) that precludes any response to God's word. They are callous, beyond feeling. Further, there is a self-induced moral degeneration that is unending, since there is *a continual lust for more.* The difference noted above between God's giving the Gentiles over to moral degeneration and the Gentiles' giving themselves over to such impurity is comparable to the situation of the Egyptian pharaoh described in Exodus. The biblical text says both that Pharaoh hardened his heart against God (Ex 8:15, 32; 9:34) and that God hardened his heart (Ex 9:12; 10:1, 20, 27; 11:10; 14:8; compare Rom 9:17-18).

The Basis for a Radical Change (4:20-24) Although the conjunction that introduces the next sentence (v. 20) is only a mild adversative, an emphatic *you* at the very beginning sets up a vivid contrast—literally, "But as for you, you did not learn Christ that way." This of course does not mean that the Gentiles learned Christ in one way and the Ephesians in another. This is Paul's way of introducing the fact that Jesus was the embodiment of truth (v. 21) in sharp contrast with the false abstractions

Nevertheless, both situations serve as a warning that resistance to God can dull, perhaps destroy, one's ability to receive his convicting and redeeming word.

of paganism. To express it in retrospect from the perspective of the church, the central truth of Christianity does not reside mainly in its creeds or sacraments but in Jesus himself.

Verse 21 describes the process of conversion: *you heard . . . and were taught*. This is pictured as an acceptance not merely of superior religious ideas or values but of Jesus himself. Without him, even theological precision is inadequate for salvation. The introductory words in the Greek assume that the Ephesians *had* heard.

Whether this singular use in Ephesians of the name *Jesus* alone, without title, has particular significance has been debated. If Paul is using it simply as our Lord's human name, it would indicate that the abstract *truth* was embodied in the man Jesus. What the Ephesians were taught unfolds in the next verse, and we are first assured that this was *in accordance with* truth in Jesus.

The teaching is, in summary, that there should be a radical difference between pre- and postconversion character. There are three verbs that depend on *were taught* (v. 22): *to put off* (v. 22), *to be made new* (v. 23) and *to put on* (v. 24). The imagery of old clothing that is taken off to be discarded and replaced with the new was common in ancient writings. The important parallel in Colossians 3:8-14 is far more extended than others in the Pauline epistles. It includes the additional idea of putting old sinful deeds to death, and it specifies a change in personal relationships as part of the new life. Galatians 3:27-28 uses the imagery of being clothed with Christ at baptism. Galatians and Colossians have something in common not found in Ephesians, the effect in social relations among believers ("neither Jew nor Greek, slave nor free, [nor is there] male [and] female" in Galatians and a slightly different series in Colossians). This imagery is not unusual in Scripture. The instruction in Ephesians is not as directly imperatival as in Colossians but assumes that the readers need only to be reminded of what they already know in order to obey it completely.

4:21 For more on the debate regarding the use of the name Jesus without title, see Lincoln 1990:281-82. He sees no particular emphasis in its use here.

4:23 The NIV translation *attitude of your minds* reflects an interpretive decision as to the meaning of *pneuma* here. This word for spirit can refer to the Holy Spirit, who certainly renews us (Tit 3:5), to the human spirit (1 Thess 5:23) or to an attitude (Phil 1:27). Since

The *old self* and *new self* have received various interpretations. One is to understand these to refer to "natures," but this can result in ontological confusion. Are there two actual persons or beings within the Christian, an old one and a new one? Is this what is meant in 2 Corinthians 5:17 as a "new creation"? Another stream of thought conceives of the *new self* (translated literally as the "new man") as Christ himself in the believer. This founders on the statement at the end of verse 24 that it is "created," which cannot be said of Christ. The concept of corporate personality, which gained popularity initially in Old Testament studies, has been applied to the old and new self. Unbelievers are collectively identified with Adam; believers are identified with Christ. Some corporate sense may indeed be present here. It seems to be present in the Colossians parallel, where, following a reference to the new self, Paul says, "Here [*hopou*, literally 'where'] there is no Greek or Jew . . ." and lists some of the social differences that are abrogated in Christ (Col 3:11). This fits a corporate sense.

Another possibility, perhaps involving fewer complications than others, is that the old self is simply the person I once was, the character I once bore, the personality that was being destroyed by sin. The new self is the new character I *put on,* the totality of Christian personal traits that is *created to be like God in true righteousness and holiness* (v. 24).

Between the putting off of verse 22 and the putting on of verse 24 stands the other content of the teaching the readers had received, mental renewal (v. 23). This is necessary because prior to conversion most of them had experienced the mental futility and darkness that characterized the unbelieving Gentiles (vv. 17-18). This renewal is apparently continual, since in contrast to the verbs of putting on and off, which are in the aorist tense, which represents simple action, this is in the present tense.

Examples of This Radical Change (4:25—5:2) Good preachers are on a continual quest for helpful illustrations. Sometimes the most

the phrase is "spirit of *your* minds," it cannot be the Holy Spirit, so it must either mean "mental attitude" or, more likely, the human spirit that guides our thoughts. Such diverse scholars as Calvin (1948:295), Bruce (1948:358) and Schnackenburg (1991:200) understand the sense to be the human spirit as renewed by the Holy Spirit.

effective are case studies, either real or hypothetical situations in which the message of the biblical text is or can be applied. Paul provides three examples, each of which is a matter of personal relationships. These are intertwined with each other and with references to God, Christ and the Holy Spirit.

Replacing Falsehood with Truth (4:25) Paul picks up the image of putting off clothing and applies it to lying. The sentence begins with *Therefore* (*dio;* NRSV "So then"). This indicates the close, logical relationship between theory and practice. The command is not merely negative, but positive. It is not enough to cease lying; *falsehood* must be replaced by truth. This is especially appropriate given the introductory statement about "the truth that is in Jesus" (v. 21). The *neighbor* in this case is presumably a Christian, given the causal clause that follows, *for we are all members of one body*. It forwards Paul's concern with the unity of the body. Falsehood divides; truth unites.

Replacing Anger with Forgiveness (4:26-27) *In your anger do not sin* is hard to understand. The issue is whether the Greek *orgizesthe* is (1) an imperative, a command to be angry (assuming an appropriate reason), (2) an imperative giving permission (go ahead and sin if you cannot help it), (3) concessive (even though you may sin) or (4) conditional (if you sin). The issue cannot be decided by grammar alone. Theology and ethics must be considered.

The explanation for option 1 is usually connected with one of two assumptions. One is that "righteous anger" is justifiable. The action of Jesus against the money changers in the temple is usually cited. However, Scripture does not describe Jesus as angry, and if he was, this is not necessarily an example for us. Also the anger ("wrath") of God mentioned in 2:3 is judicial and truly righteous. The other assumption sometimes made is that anger is healthy for a person and should not always be suppressed. Whether or not that is true, it is not taught here. The explanation for option 2 is that anger is wrong but inevitable. Take the first step of anger, but not the second step of maintaining that attitude. This interpretation would put Paul in the

_____

4:25 The NIV's *for we are members of one body* where the Greek has *allēlōn melē*

position of tolerating sin. The explanation for option 3 is that anger is wrong and is not to be encouraged. Nevertheless, in the event it happens, it should not be allowed to fester. The explanation for option 4 is that anger is an emotion and one must simply accept it.

The translation "Be angry . . ." in the KJV and NRSV seems to reflect option 1 or 2. The interpretation in the paraphrase by Eugene H. Peterson is that anger is a good thing deserving of commendation: "Go ahead and be angry. You do well to be angry . . ." (Peterson 1993). This is clearly a strong form of category 1. The Revised English Bible's "If you are angry . . ." represents option 4, or possibly 3. The NIV's *In your anger* seems to assume anger in the sense of 4. Actually it brings the clause into conformity with the NIV wording of its source, Psalm 4:4, "In your anger do not sin."

The context of Psalm 4 should yield some clue as to its use there, though the interpretation of that verse in the psalm is itself difficult. When Psalm 4 is seen as consisting of alternating sections, with verse 1 being the call of believers to God, verse 2 God's call to unbelievers, verse 3 assurance to believers, verses 4-5 an exhortation to unbelievers and verses 6-7 the resolution of the believers' perplexity through trust in God, the meaning of the troublesome clause begins to unfold. The exhortation to unbelievers begins with an expression that could signify anger or trembling. In either case, they should progress from their antagonism to reflection and then conversion.

If this is the sequence of thought in its original setting, Paul's use of it could be parallel. In Ephesians 4:25 the convert is to forsake falsehood and in verse 28 to forsake stealing. Between these is the exhortation of verses 26-27 to forsake anger. The new converts pictured in 4:17—5:2 are clearly in progress. At their present stage they are still tempted to be angry. Even if this happens, they should be careful not to allow that anger to fester, to last beyond nightfall and become an opportunity for the devil to use for evil.

Thus the meaning of the troublesome phrase in verse 26 would be best represented by option 3 above. Anger (except for righteous anger, such as God's wrath) is wrong. It is a Christian virtue to control it, or

("members of one another") reflects an understanding that the *neighbor* is a believer and that it is the body of Christ that is implied.

more properly, the Spirit produces such virtues as patience (Gal 5:22). But even when anger gets out of control, its duration must be limited by the setting sun—practical as well as spiritual advice.

The reference to the devil (v. 27) informs us that there are various ways besides obvious direct attack in which Satan works against the Lord and his people. In this case a strained relationship provides the occasion. Given the emphasis in Ephesians on reconciliation and unity, this is an important fact to understand.

Replacing Stealing with Giving (4:28) Along with falsehood and anger, the next "case" of needed changes in the life of a new Christian is to forsake *stealing.* Once again, it is not merely a negative step, avoidance of a sin, but a positive one, replacing stealing with useful work. In this case a second positive instruction follows: to have *something to share with those in need.*

One could easily pass this by with a nod of agreement, but it deserves a second look for three reasons. One is that stealing is a major problem in contemporary society; another is that financial responsibility is of immense importance to Paul; a third is that stealing is forbidden in the Ten Commandments.

One of life's little embarrassments comes when one leaves a store and hears the theft alarm go off because some item purchased was not properly desensitized. That momentary circumstance is minor compared with the immense amount of money lost today by stores, libraries and other businesses—to say nothing of victimized individuals—through theft. Shoplifting has grown to immense proportions. We in the West have grown accustomed to seeing surveillance cameras peeping at us in stores, banks and other business establishments. One might hope that enough conversions would solve the problem, but if that were the case Paul would not have had to write this passage, for it is to those already converted that he addresses it.

Paul had a strong personal work ethic. He wrote the Corinthians that he had the right to receive financial remuneration for his preaching but refused to do so (1 Cor 9:3-18). He reminded the Thessalonians that he

---

4:29 The NIV's *according to their needs* and the NRSV's "as there is need" are attempts to translate an awkward Greek construction, *pros oikodomēn tēs chreias,* literally, "for building up of the need." Obviously it could hardly mean that the need itself is to be

worked day and night so as not to burden anyone (1 Thess 2:6-9). In part, at least, his reason for working at a craft while he was preaching was to demonstrate his genuine motives, in contrast to the greed of many wandering pagan preachers of his day. But he also did this as "a model" for Christians to follow (2 Thess 3:9). He believed strongly that all believers should work for a living and not be idle, offering as a principle "Anyone unwilling to work should not eat" (2 Thess 3:10 NRSV). We would assume that this principle is in his mind as he writes to the Ephesians, but he is dealing with more than a refusal to work or an unhealthy dependence on other people. While working and giving are the desired outcomes, the problem is stealing. And that must be dealt with if the desired outcomes are to follow.

Therefore we can assume, given Paul's reverence for the Law, that a prime reason for his command not to steal is that it is one of the Ten Commandments: "You shall not steal" (Ex 20:15). The Old Testament elsewhere advocates giving to those in need, especially in the year for canceling debts (Deut 15). And Paul encouraged such giving so that "there might be equality" (2 Cor 8:13). Both the negative and the positive aspects of this verse are therefore important: give up stealing; work with your hands; give to those who have need.

Replacing Unwholesome Talk with That Which Edifies (4:29)
The sequence of "cases" continues with yet another example of the substitution of the good for the bad. *Unwholesome* is a translation of the Greek word *sapros,* which was used to describe something that is foul, putrid, decaying or rotten. The mention of salt with regard to speech in Colossians 4:6 may suggest a preservative function, in which case it would highlight Paul's sense here of the decomposing effect of bad language (Lincoln 1990:305). The use of a word suggesting decay is all the more striking when we realize that "this is the one place in the New Testament where it is used of anything other than material things mostly in a state of decomposition" (Morris 1994:146).

It is probably not only the language we use but also the content of

augmented, which would be the case if *chreias* were an objective genitive, so it must be understood as a compressed expression, perhaps meaning "whatever is needy" or "wherever [or whenever] there is need."

what we say that has this effect. The reasons for thinking that *unwhole-some* refers to content are (1) the alternative is *building others up*, so there must be some content in the bad speech that tears people down (Bruce 1984:362-63), and (2) the injunctions that follow in verses 31-32 have to do with attitudes toward others, which shows that Paul is concerned with what our talk does to others, not just the language we use.

All this calls to mind Jesus' teaching in the context of the Beelzebub controversy. He said that we are judged by our words, which could be misunderstood as a superficial basis for judgment, especially since words can be careless: "[people will] have to give account on the day of judgment for every careless word they have spoken" (Mt 12:36). The fact is, however, that words—even or perhaps especially careless ones—reveal the nature of their source, the human heart. Jesus made this clear with the familiar tree and fruit imagery (Mt 12:33-35).

The whole pattern of our speech is important. Increasingly one hears even religious people using the name of God carelessly. Foul language and dirty jokes are common, and they are frequently used now on TV and in movies. And if we are to understand Paul's warning in the larger sense of whatever tends to tear people down, it certainly would apply to demeaning comments and gossip. It is a sad fact that at the close of the twentieth century politeness waned in the U.S. Congress, and on American streets it became smart to "diss" others and in general to have an "in your face" attitude.

The Christian substitute for all this is what helps edify others. The wording here, *what is helpful for building others up according to their needs, that it may benefit those who listen* is somewhat similar to Romans 15:2, "Each of us should please his neighbor for his good, to build him up." The sequence of thought in these passages is that conversation should *benefit* others, and that benefit is defined as what builds them up. Whereas Ephesians 4:12 refers to the building up of the "body," here the picture is of individual growth. Just as the former thief now helps in cases of need, so the person who formerly offended others with inappropriate language now meets their need. The speech of those who have received God's transforming grace now is always to be characterized by grace (Col 4:6) and should *benefit,* literally "give grace to," others. This does not mean that our words are a means of saving grace, but that they enrich the lives of others.

Refraining from Grieving the Holy Spirit (4:30) This is an unexpected command in this context, though it is not necessarily a "stray element," as Markus Barth called it (1974b:447). On the contrary, it can be understood as a summary of the preceding teaching about words. If we tear down others by our speech and by the attitudes betrayed by our speech, we are grieving the Spirit who indwells us and by whom we *were sealed for the day of redemption.*

Many people, when thinking about the end of history and God's final dealing with the human race, think only in terms of judgment. While there is judgment ahead for the unbeliever and evaluation of the believer's life at the judgment seat of Christ (2 Cor 5:10), the believer's sins have already been judged at the cross. What we look forward to is the *day* when God will complete his redemptive work. Peter describes this as "the coming of the salvation that is ready to be revealed in the last time" (1 Pet 1:5). See Ephesians 1:14 on God's perspective, the redemption of his possession.

The words *grieving the Holy Spirit* are an allusion to Isaiah 63:9-11:

In all their distress he too was distressed,

and the angel of his presence saved [compare Eph 2:8] them.

In his love and mercy [compare Eph 2:4] he redeemed them. . . .

Yet they rebelled

and grieved his Holy Spirit [compare Eph 4:30].

So he turned and became their enemy

and he himself fought against them.

Then his people recalled the days of old,

the days of Moses and his people—

where is he who brought them through the sea,

with the shepherd of his flock?

Where is he who set

his Holy Spirit among them . . . ?

If Paul intended to convey something of the sense of the context in Isaiah, the thought might be that the lost condition of the Ephesians "distressed" God, and they should be careful, now that they are saved, not to grieve God's Spirit by failure to fulfill the radical changes God expects of them. Just as God "redeemed" his ancient people, so he has sealed the Ephesian believers for the *day of redemption* (Eph 4:30). They belong to him, and as the Spirit has assumed responsibility to keep them in God's ownership, so Christians are responsible to live in a way that pleases their Owner and Guardian.

Replacing Malice with Forgiveness (4:31—5:2) Victims and observers of strife between Christians are well aware of the need addressed here. Honesty requires the acknowledgment that at times what is presented as a doctrinal concern is at heart a hostile attitude toward the person accused. Even apart from such a public stance, those who profess faith in Christ sometimes have underlying feelings about others in the church that can poison relationships and continue to do so generation through generation.

Ephesians 4:31—5:2 comprises a series of vivid words about hostility set in contrast to each other. Paul had earlier spoken of anger; now he condemns *every form of malice,* specifying also *bitterness, rage and anger, brawling and slander.* The words cover a variety of strong hostile attitudes. They stand in polar opposition to the attitudes encouraged in 4:2.

Forgiveness is not the only positive element that should replace the hostile attitudes just described. It stands third in the series: *kind . . . compassionate . . . forgiving.* The first two are adjectives, the third a participle. In the Greek "Be to one another" precedes the group, and "one another" follows it, serving as the object of *forgiving.* Kindness and compassion marked God's attitude to those who deserved wrath in 2:4, 7, where the same word as used here, *kindness,* appears. These qualities are also in 4:2, where they are marked for adoption as strongly as their opposites are marked for dismissal here in verse 31. It is the attitudes of grace, mercy, kindness and compassion that make forgiveness possible in our relationships.

These attitudes should make forgiveness what it ought to be, not merely "letting bygones be bygones." Forgiveness is not merely dismissing something out of mind, trying to forget it or overlooking it. A great deal of harm can be done not only when Christians perpetuate resentful attitudes against those who have wronged them but also when they sweep these wrongs "under the carpet," where they stay unresolved. We must face our own attitudes as well as the wrongs of others. If we truly forgive another that means putting an end to the matter by forgiving just as God has forgiven us, acknowledging the wrong and its effect on us, and then dismissing it, no longer pressing judgment and never calling it back to mind. Jesus taught that it is the person who has been forgiven much who loves much (Lk 7:47). It helps us to forgive others to remember how much God has forgiven us and the price that was paid. True forgiveness will mean that even if in our humanity we cannot completely forget the actions and effects that someone's sin caused, we can forgive the sin itself and refrain from allowing it to affect our estimation of that person.

Such forgiveness, however, requires more than a good attitude. It requires a deep sense of one's own forgiveness by God and the clear example provided by the sacrifice of Christ, as demonstrated in 4:32—5:2. There are three modes of comparison here, a comparative adverb that is repeated and, between those two occurrences, a noun *(imitators)* implying comparison:

Just as [kathōs] in Christ God forgave you. (4:32)

Be imitators of God . . . as dearly loved children. (5:1)

Just as [kathōs] Christ loved us. (5:2)

Christians sometimes speak of the "imitation of Christ," especially with reference to the classic work of that name by Thomas à Kempis. In contemporary usage the word "imitation" conjures up pictures of false products, mere second-rate copies of an original, if not counterfeits. In the Greco-Roman world, however, imitation *(mimēsis)* was a commendable enterprise, an attempt to follow the best examples. So Paul wrote, "Follow my example, as I follow the example of Christ" (1 Cor 11:1). More recently, one of the most widely published and influential books of the early twentieth century was *In His Steps* by Charles Sheldon. In any situation, Sheldon maintained, one may ask, "What would Jesus have done in this circumstance?" In the present passage both God and Christ are presented as the worthy objects of imitation. We should behave *just as* God did in his forgiveness and *just as* Christ did in his sacrifice on the cross. Ephesians 2:4 describes the love and mercy of God to those who deserved wrath, and 2:7 points to eternity ahead, when God will further reveal his grace "expressed in his kindness to us in Christ Jesus."

Another important word pattern, overlapping the first, features *love:*

As *dearly loved* children . . . (5:1)

Live a life of love. (5:2)

Just as Christ loved us . . . (5:2)

The sequence itself carries a message: We are loved, we live in love, we follow the example of Christ, whose love led to self-sacrifice. The last clause, *and gave himself up for us as a fragrant offering and sacrifice to God,* prepares for the kind of love a husband should have for his wife (5:25).

The middle member, *Live a life of love,* employs the verb *peripateō,* which in earlier English translations was commonly translated "walk." The verb and its tense (present aspect) imply a continuing pattern of life. *Fragrant offering* recalls the pleasure of God in Old Testament sacrifices, a pleasure that is, of course, infinitely enhanced with the sacrifice of the beloved Son. Since God was pleased with the offering of his Son, we can please him by having the same attitude. This does not mean, of course, that we can achieve salvation for others (or ourselves) by some sacrificial act. It does mean that giving ourselves lovingly, and at some personal cost, for the good of others and for the glory of God is pleasing to him. Hebrews 13:16 demonstrates this: "And do not forget to do good and to share with others, for with such sacrifices God is pleased."

The Need for Further Moral Changes (5:3-14) Of all the areas of life that can be ruined by sin, it is sad that the most intimate relationship, the sexual—with all its potential for beauty, joy and fulfillment—is so vulnerable, so easily ruined and so prone to bring public disrepute. It is also unfortunate that pastors and other Christian leaders are suscep- tible to distortion of the counseling and other close associations char- acteristic of religious ministry. But there are other circumstances as well to which the tenth commandment, with its prohibition of covetousness, applies. So greed appears along with sexual immorality and other

---

5:2 *Peripateō* is found a number of times in Paul's writings (though not in the Pastoral Epistles) and conveys the figurative sense, known from other ancient writings, of a way of life. In Ephesians it occurs eight times: 2:2, where NIV translates it "followed the ways" (of

impurity in the instructions of Ephesians 5:3. Whether that greed is for money or for food, or (more likely in this context) for sexual gratification from someone else's spouse, it is contrary to God's will and can constitute idolatry (v. 5).

Paul calls on Christians, who must live in a manner worthy of their calling (4:1) and who should love as their Savior did (4:32—5:2), to avoid a manner of life that is not proper for *God's holy people* (5:3). In the Old Testament God's holiness required the holiness of his people, who had to keep a number of commands and prohibitions to demonstrate that holiness. Some of these seem irrelevant to moral purity. Their significance lies more in their identification of the people who belong to God (for example, Lev 19:1-37, which following the statement "Be holy because I, the LORD your God, am holy" incorporates such different commands as "Do not lie" and "Do not wear clothing woven of two kinds of material"). In the Ephesians 5 context, *sexual immorality* and *coarse joking* (v. 4) are both serious offenses for God's holy people, not only as symbols of the distinction between what is appropriate and what is not before a holy God, but as vices that are in themselves wrong.

Readers of ancient moralistic writings would have been familiar with lists of vices and virtues. Verse 4 contains a brief list of the kinds of speech that should not be on the lips of Christians. They overlap in meaning; all of them relate to what we might call "dirty language" or "dirty jokes." Apparently in that society, as is the case in our own, suggestive language was a way of introducing sexual overtones that might not be accepted in straightforward conversation. This might constitute the *hint of sexual immorality* Paul speaks of in verse 3. The substitute that Paul prescribes for such obscenity is *thanksgiving*. Desire comes out of dissatisfaction with what we have. Thanksgiving, on the other hand, not only expresses satisfaction but, in a sense, can even create satisfaction within us.

The need for serious moral change now receives its strongest argument (vv. 5-6): our eternal destiny. We are accustomed to various kinds of appeals preachers use to motivate people to be converted to

this world); 2:10 (good works), "to do"; 4:1, "live a life"; 4:17, "live"; 4:17, (as the Gentiles) "do"; 5:2, *live* (the passage before us now); 5:8, "live"; and 5:15, "live."

Christ. But beyond the invitation to peace, a fulfilled life, the joy of salvation and so forth, there is a starkly different kind of approach that one does not hear often anymore. That is the threat of unending separation from God, of eternal loneliness, of blackest darkness forever (Jude 13 regarding apostates), in short, of hell itself. This reality should, if declared in the proper manner in the power of God, turn people to Christ. In this letter to believers, however, the author introduces the fate of those who practice such vices as those listed in verses 3-4. These vices are not to be tolerated in the Christian community, nor are Christians to be *partners* with those who practice them.

The argument is that those who commit such sins, who are described as *immoral, impure, greedy* and *idolaters,* will be excluded from the *kingdom* and are destined to experience the *wrath* of God. The argument is strengthened by the structure:

A. Command (vv. 3-4): Do not allow any of the vices among yourselves.

B. Basis for command A (v. 5): Be sure of this:

1. Such people, the *immoral* and *impure,* are actually idolaters.

2. They are doomed to exclusion.

B'. Basis for command A' (v. 6): Do not be deceived:

1. Such people are *disobedient.*

2. They will suffer God's *wrath* (v. 6).

A'. Command (v. 7): Therefore do not be their *partners.*

The word *gar (for)* appears in both verse 5 and verse 6, expressing reasons for the commands. The injunctions (B and B') "Be sure of this" (NRSV) and "Do not be deceived" emphasize the importance of knowing the consequence of such immorality. The three adjectives *immoral, impure* and *greedy* correspond to the three words in noun form in verse 3. Sexual lust is not the only kind of excessive desire addressed here, but it is the dominant one.

The importance of *thanksgiving* in verse 4 can be further seen in that a lack of thanksgiving is a failure to acknowledge God as the giver of every "good and perfect gift" (Jas 1:17). Instead of that acknowledgment, the sinful human tendency is to focus on the gift alone and to desire it not only apart from God but instead of God. To substitute anything (or anyone) as the object of our desire and (the natural consequence) the object of our worship for God is idolatry. Therefore such a person— specifically the *greedy person,* but Paul is perhaps referring to the others described as well—is an *idolater.* The Ten Commandments begin with the command against idolatry and conclude with the command against covetousness (Ex 20:3, 17). The two are brought together full circle when we understand from verse 5 that greed is idolatry. That is clear also from the list in Colossians 3:5, "sexual immorality, impurity, lust, evil desires and greed, which is idolatry."

The terms *idolater* (v. 5; see B[1]) and *disobedient* (v. 6; see B [1]) reveal the fact that it is not just the actions of these people but who they are in the depth of their being that calls for judgment. That judgment comprises (1) exclusion from *any inheritance in the kingdom of Christ and of God* (v. 5; see B[2]) and (2) God's *wrath* (v. 6; see B [2]). Regarding the first, the terminology ascribing the kingdom to both Christ and God is unusual for Paul and may be intended to emphasize the present as well as future aspects of the kingdom that are denied to these idolaters (Bruce 1984:372; compare Lincoln 1990:325). They will have nothing of all the great and wonderful blessings of the reign of God. If the first aspect of the judgment brings thoughts of isolation and deprivation, the second brings fearful thoughts of experiencing the deserved anger of our righteous God. When we realize that such doom is the destiny specifically of those who are *disobedient,* we understand that it is not a judgment on people who did not know better.

The double description, *idolaters* and *disobedient,* and the double condemnation, exclusion from the *kingdom* and *God's wrath,* are therefore extremely forceful. Readers must take this into account as they hear that they are neither to allow the described behavior nor to enter into partnership (v. 7) with the perpetrators.

Verse 8 begins with a reminder that the readers, most of whom were formerly unbelieving Gentiles, *were once darkness.* The wording is unexpected. To say not that they were merely *in* darkness but that they *were* darkness is startling. In parallel to this they are now *light* (again, not just *in* light).

At the beginning of this section, the contrast between darkness and light occurs within the familiar *once* and *now* construction used so effectively in 2:11-22. The two images following this, however, are strange to the modern ear: *children of light* and *fruit of the light*. As for the first, *children of light* is an idiomatic expression familiar to the original readers, especially Jewish readers. It was a way of expressing people's character or destiny. A contrasting phrase in the same idiom occurs in verse 6, where *those who are disobedient* (NIV) is a translation of the original "sons of disobedience" (compare the same phrase in 2:2), and in 2:3, where the original phrase is "children of wrath" (NIV *objects of wrath*). The theme of light and darkness appears frequently in Scripture and is prominent in the Dead Sea Scrolls. The Gospel of John picks this up and in 12:36 has a phrase comparable to *children of light* in Ephesians 5:8: "Put your trust in the light while you have it, so that you may become sons of light."

Fruit of the light is also an unusual phrase. "Fruit of the Spirit" (Gal 5:22-23) is more familiar and perhaps more understandable. It is easier to think of a person, the Spirit of God or a human being, rather than impersonal, lifeless light, as producing *fruit*. Yet even before the knowledge of photosynthesis, people knew that plants need light to grow and bear fruit. Also, given the identification of God himself as light (1 Jn 1:5), it is not an impersonal or lifeless light that produces fruit in believers. John 1:4 supports this association of life and light: "In him was life, and that life was the light of men." In his first letter John tells us to "walk in the light" (1 Jn 1:7); here Paul tells us to *live as children of light* (Eph 5:8). Verse 9 explains the reason for this, and verses 10-14 explain how to do it. Light, then, has ethical meaning and existential meaning: "it means well-being" (Barth 1974b:600).

Goodness, righteousness and truth (v. 9), which constitute the *fruit of the light,* are comprehensive virtues. They express desirable moral qualities taught throughout Scripture. Micah 6:8 expresses the kind of life that is in view when it shows that God is not satisfied with mere ritual but has showed us "what is good. And what does the LORD require of you? To act justly and to love mercy and to walk humbly with your God." *Goodness* is a basic moral virtue, *righteousness* conveys perhaps more specifically doing what is proper and just, and *truth* expresses a wholeness or integrity that goes beyond merely saying what is true.

The fact that the reader is to *find out what pleases the Lord* indicates that this list is not exhaustive but rather gives direction for those desiring to produce the *fruit of the light*. Generation after generation of Christians has tried to provide their children and new converts with instructions on the spiritual life. Each generation has its own real-life moral context, and often each forms a list of what is evil or what is good in terms of that limited context. Over the past century or so such diverse practices as bobbing women's hair, wearing above-the-knee bathing suits, going to movies, shopping on Sunday and women's attending college have appeared on vice lists. While we do need to apply biblical principles in specific terms, such lists tend to be limited and irrelevant in other moral situations.

Nevertheless, Scripture itself provides lists of vices and ideals, including a number in Paul's writing, which can be compared with similar lists in secular moral writings. Examples of good and bad conduct (such as the "acts of the sinful nature" and the "fruit of the Spirit" in Galatians 5:19-23, as well as the kinds of behavior described in the present passage) help the reader to identify such conduct in their own lives. The examples are mainly inner moral traits that can surface in any society and produce either good deeds or misdeeds that are distinctive in that social setting. To think otherwise distorts the nature of Christian morality and produces rigid codifications that have to be revised with the next set of social conditions.

To *find out what pleases the Lord* does not mean that God makes it difficult for us to know what he wants. Rather, we should test carefully whatever we consider doing to be sure he would approve. The word for *find out* can mean both to test and to approve. God wants us to approve what he would approve, that is, what *pleases* him. The form of the verb (a participle, "find*ing* out") can be taken as a command but also, and perhaps more likely, describes what the Ephesians are already doing.

Sometimes one tests and *dis*approves. If we find that certain practices come under the category of *the fruitless deeds of darkness,* we are to *have nothing to do with* them. These are the alternative to the *fruit of the light* in verse 9. There the deeds themselves are the fruit; here the deeds should produce the fruit but fail to do so; they are *fruitless.* In verse 7 the command is not to be partners with those who are disobedient; here it is not to share in what they do. Therefore we may now understand that verse 7 does not mean that we should be uncivil to those who are disobedient but that we should not participate with them in their disobedience.

Verse 11 concludes *but rather expose them,* and verse 12 gives as a reason for exposing them that it is *shameful even to mention* them. The obvious question is how to expose something without even mentioning it. Furthermore, Christians have sometimes disagreed as to whether they should name sins, especially those of a sexual nature, publicly. One possible solution is to consider that while the deeds may be the same in both verses, the latter ones are dealt with in a manner appropriate to the secrecy of their performance. They are *what the disobedient do in secret* and should be kept in secret. It should be kept in mind that the word *for* introduces the whole Greek sentence beginning in verse 12 (Morris 1994:168). Another solution is to realize that to expose the deeds does not require talking about them. It requires introducing the light that can display the contrast between good and evil and that can, to change the metaphor, shrivel up the evil deeds. The third solution is that it is a matter of motive. To discuss evil deeds, even in the form of *foolish talk* and jokes (v. 4), can be a sordid way of focusing on them. But the purpose of exposing them in the sense of verse 11 is to destroy them. The intention, as well as the result, is appropriate.

Verse 13 tells us that light makes whatever is *exposed* to it visible. In contrast, that which is plunged into darkness is invisible to the eye, so evil deeds that are practiced in secret are not seen. But when such evil is exposed by God's light it *becomes visible* (v. 13). The first part of verse 14 functions as a transition from being exposed by the light to what we might describe as being "transformed" by that light. An object that is

---

5:14 The first part of this verse is notoriously difficult. One of the factors that complicate the interpretation is the substantival participle *phaneroumenon,* the voice of which could be understood either as middle ("that which makes visible") or passive ("that which is made visible"). If middle, it means "That which makes visible is light." NIV reverses the verbal order, *for it is light that makes everything visible.* This puts the emphasis on the effectiveness of the light, and this is appropriate in the context, since later in the verse it is Christ who shines on the believer. On the other hand, NRSV understands the verb as passive: "for everything that becomes visible is light." It could be argued that the latter construction

illumined not only becomes visible but may also take on luminosity (v. 14). That is, it glows as though it were the source of light itself (compare v. 8). The progress of thought at the end of this section is fairly clear, though the precise meaning of the first part of verse 14 is disputed. The climax in verse 14 is the promise that those who awake will, on rising from death, receive the light of Christ.

Hymns and other kinds of Christian songs have tremendous impact not only on those who sing but also on those who listen. In the second part of verse 14 the text includes a song directed not to God but to the listener. It is customary to consider this a baptismal hymn. Whether it is or not does not affect its interpretation or application. While baptism represents dying and rising with Christ (Rom 6:4), this hymn seems to speak not so much to the person who has already trusted Christ as to those either observing the baptism or hearing the song later, for the subject is not only rising from the dead but also awakening from sleep. If that is the case, this could be considered the first gospel song of which we have a record. *This is why it is said* indicates that the quote is part of the early Christian tradition, cited by divine inspiration in this biblical text. The same formula *(dio legei)* occurs in 4:8, where it introduces Scripture. Characteristics indicating that this is a song include the structure (parallel ideas: *wake up . . . rise up*), the rhythm and the use of similar-sounding endings to the first two lines *(ho katheudōn . . . ek tōn nekrōn)*.

The Need for the Filling of the Spirit (5:15-21) The series of contrasts between good and evil continues, but with the fundamental addition of the role of the Holy Spirit. The passage may be structured as follows:

    Be very careful, then, how you live—

    Contrast 1:   *not as unwise*

---

follows naturally from the passive *elenchomena* ("exposed") in the previous clause (v. 13). Another complicating factor is that the verb *exposed* implies the uncovering of something evil, while the Christian's experience in verse 14 shows that being "illuminated" has a beneficial effect. Perhaps there is a subtle transition in the author's mind in which what the light initially exposes as evil it also transforms into good, that is, into *light* itself. The exegetical commentaries always address this issue, but there is also a clear, though very brief, discussion in connection with interpretive issues relating to the Greek voices in Moule 1959:25.

> *but as wise,*
>> *making the most of every opportunity,*
>> *because the days are evil.*

Contrast 2:   *Therefore do not be foolish,*
>> *but understand what the Lord's will is.*

Contrast 3:   *Do not get drunk on wine,*
>> *which leads to debauchery.*
>> *Instead, be filled with the Spirit.*
>>> *Speak to one another with psalms, hymns and*
>>> *spiritual songs.*
>>> *Sing*
>>>> *and make music in your heart to the Lord,*
>>>> *always giving thanks to God the Father for*
>>>> *everything,*
>>>>> *in the name of our Lord Jesus Christ.*
>>> *Submit to one another out of reverence for Christ.*

The Need to Be Wise (5:15-17) Although "wisdom literature" is significant in Scripture, notably in Proverbs, with proverbial sayings scattered throughout the Gospels, in James and elsewhere, Christians tend to miss the importance and value of such teachings. Those who love the Lord are rightly concerned to do his will but often in seeking it fail to give sufficient place to the wisdom God has already made available. He has provided this primarily through the Scriptures, not only through individual verses but in the accumulation of teaching about himself, the world, the church. This includes what Scripture says about us both as limited, sinful human brings and as Christians. But wisdom is more than knowledge, even Bible knowledge. It is knowing God, maturing in our relationship with him and walking with him so closely and perceptively that we are enabled to develop a godly character, live thoughtfully and make proper choices in life. Through the revelation that God has given us of his own nature and of the ways he has acted in human history, we can usually gain insight as to how God would view the various ethical and moral choices that confront us. In spite of our sinful nature, we are blessed with the

---

5:15-21 There is a verb in each of the indented lines following the command to be filled with the Spirit. These are all translations of Greek participles (dependent on the main

ability to make choices wisely. Such a mature knowledge of God and his Word should help us to go beyond the tendency to extract verses out of context and apply them mechanically to life's decisions or to become overly concerned with seeking special supernatural leading.

The exhortation in verses 15-17 to live wisely, to make the most of every opportunity and to understand what the Lord's will is can be obeyed, because God has already given us the necessary resources in the biblical wisdom passages and in the revelation of God's holy nature. We are therefore able to process life's decisions wisely. If we do not have the needed wisdom, then we can request this from God (Jas 1:5).

There are two parallels to Ephesians 5:15-17 in Colossians:

Let the word of Christ dwell in you richly as you teach and admonish one another with all wisdom, and as you sing psalms, hymns and spiritual songs with gratitude in your hearts to God. And whatever you do, whether in word or deed, do it all in the name of the Lord Jesus, giving thanks to God the Father through him. (Col 3:16-17)

Be wise in the way you act toward outsiders; make the most of every opportunity. (Col 4:5)

It is not difficult to see the close verbal parallels between Colossians 4:5 and Ephesians 5:15-16. Both have the Greek *peripateite*, "walk," and Ephesians has *as wise* while the Greek of Colossians 4:5 has "in wisdom," a minor difference. *Make the most of every opportunity* (literally, "buying up the time") follows in both. The major difference is the context. The Colossians passage occurs after the "household code" (instructions to wives, husbands and so on), whereas the Ephesians passage precedes it. In Colossians 4:5 Paul is concerned with "outsiders." He requests prayer for his preaching (Col 4:2-4); that request immediately precedes the injunction to walk wisely. That injunction adds "in the way you act toward outsiders," which does not occur in Ephesians. Furthermore, Colossians 4:5 is followed by "Let your conversation be always full of grace, seasoned with salt, so that you may know how to answer everyone." Whereas in Ephesians the parallel section follows a long

---

verb, *be filled*): "speaking," "singing," "making music," *giving thanks* and "submitting." Since a participle can express a command, NIV translates four of the verbs as such.

denunciation of immorality and especially obscene speech, in Colossians it relates to our relationship with outsiders and how we respond to their questions.

While it is perhaps useful to speculate on the issue of literary dependency, the more profitable task of the reader is to understand and apply each passage in its own context. Colossians counsels the reader how to speak to the unbelieving world; Ephesians deals more with how to live a pure life in that world. The *opportunity* Christians are to seize should be understood within the purpose of each context. In Colossians it seems to be the opportunity to witness for Christ. Believers not only should be "wise" in relationships with "outsiders" but specifically should let their conversation be "full of grace" and "seasoned with salt." While Ephesians counsels careful speech in another passage (4:29—5:2) and while overt witnessing may certainly be assumed in 5:15-16, that is not explicitly stated. The reason given, *because the days are evil,* seems to encompass a broader circumstance, the evil nature of this present age. Christians must seize the day and accomplish God's will, which the next verse will encourage us to understand. We are to "buy" (which implies giving up what is necessary in order to own and use well) the "time" (in the sense of appropriate season or opportunity).

The Need to Be Filled (5:18) Christians who long for a deeper spiritual life and an experience of spiritual power look to Ephesians 5:18, on the filling of the Spirit, as a major text. This is not only the desire of Christians but the desire of God for us. The fact that the verb is in the passive mood indicates that while it is a command, something we are responsible to fulfill, it is something that we *allow* God to do for us. That is not only a matter of ability (we cannot fill ourselves; only God can do that) but a matter of right (we belong to God, and he has the right to fill us). In 1:13 the Holy Spirit is God's seal on us, the mark of ownership. In 4:30 this sealing is the reason we should not grieve the Spirit. We have seen that Ephesians emphasizes God's initiative in the work of salvation. We are the product of his grace. It is therefore consistent with the teaching of Ephesians that we regard the filling and control of the Holy Spirit to be God's sovereign right in our lives.

One often hears a Christian leader described as "Spirit-filled." It may be asked whether anyone other than an inspired writer of Scripture can have certain knowledge whether another Christian is indeed filled with the Spirit. Certainly Luke had knowledge by inspiration of Jesus' being full of the Spirit and led by the Spirit into the desert (Lk 4:1). In Luke 4:18 Jesus applies Isaiah's experience to himself ("The Spirit of the Lord is on me"). And in Acts, again by inspiration, Luke describes some of the early Christians as "full" of the Spirit: "Brothers, choose seven men from among you who are known to be full of the Spirit and wisdom. We will turn this responsibility over to them. . . . This proposal pleased the whole group. They chose Stephen, a man full of faith and of the Holy Spirit; also Philip, Procorus, Nicanor, Timon, Parmenas, and Nicolas from Antioch, a convert to Judaism" (Acts 6:3, 5). "But Stephen, full of the Holy Spirit, looked up to heaven and saw the glory of God, and Jesus standing at the right hand of God" (Acts 7:55). "[Barnabas] was a good man, full of the Holy Spirit and faith, and a great number of people were brought to the Lord" (Acts 11:24).

But it is not only the inspired biblical author who knows who is filled with the Spirit. The church needed to identify such people in Acts 6:3, so there must have been some unmistakable outward evidence that we can continue to recognize today. To be accurate we must note that Acts 6 does not say "filled" but "full," as though this was the effect of the inner filling of the Spirit. The resultant ministry and character of the Spirit-filled individuals was evident to those around them.

Certainly Jesus was always full of the Spirit, so in the three instances in Luke 4 he was apparently filled and led (both in 4:1) and then empowered (4:14) in a special way. The descriptions of the seven men as "full of the Spirit" in Acts seem to refer to the individuals' Christlike spiritual state or character rather than to a specific empowering.

In Ephesians the impression given by the aspect of the verb (present, implying continual or habitual action) is that while it is something the Spirit does, it is also something that we allow to be done (passive voice) continually. This blends the special work of the Spirit with an attitude of continual obedience that allows the Spirit to do this, which could be described as a spiritual state or character.

Observing the contexts where words about filling and fullness occur in Ephesians and in the companion epistle to the Colossians helps us understand this further. The verb "fill" (*plēroō*) occurs four times in

Ephesians (1:23; 3:19; 4:10; 5:18). In the first two instances it is accompanied by the noun "fullness" *(plērōma)*. In 1:23 the body of Christ, the church, is "the fullness of him who fills everything in every way." In 3:19 we are to "be filled to the measure of all the fullness of God." The verb "fill" occurs in Colossians in 1:9, 25; 2:10; 4:17, and the noun "fullness" in 1:19 and 2:9, where it is connected with the person of Christ. It is believers who are filled in two Colossians passages: "fill you with the knowledge of his will" in 1:9 and "you have been given fullness in Christ" in 2:10.

From these various references we may draw the following inferences.

1. The filling, leading and power of the Spirit were important in the life of Jesus and of the early church.

2. The fullness of God was in Christ (Col 1:19; 2:9). Christ is head of the church, and the church "is his body, the fullness of him who fills everything in every way" (Eph 1:23). Therefore the filling and fullness of the Spirit are part of the "filling" work of God and Christ. This is not just a matter of receiving blessing or of empowerment for service, but it is God functioning in our lives. We are his temple (1 Cor 3:16; 6:19), the New Testament equivalent of the tabernacle and temple where God manifested his glory: "I looked and saw the glory of the LORD filling the temple" (Ezek 44:4; compare 43:5; Is 6:1; Hag 2:7; see Arnold 1989:82-85). Being filled with the Holy Spirit therefore is a sacred responsibility appropriate to those who profess to glorify God.

3. Where Ephesians has "be filled with the Spirit," Colossians (in the parallel context of Col 3:16) has "let the word of Christ dwell in you richly." When we compare this with Paul's prayer in Colossians 1:9, "asking God to fill you with the knowledge of his will through all spiritual wisdom and understanding," we realize that the filling of the Holy Spirit is not some isolated experience but is related to understanding and doing God's will. Colossians 3:16 means that Christians would let the word of Christ (Jesus' teachings) reside in and among them as his people when they "paid heed to what they heard, bowed to its authority, assimilated its lessons, and translated them into daily living" (Bruce 1984:157-58).

These three inferences lead us to the conclusion that we should be able to discern who is "full of the Holy Spirit," because (1) Christians in the New Testament church could make that identification, (2) it is not simply an inner private experience but is the mark of a "temple" consecrated to the God who makes his glorious presence known, and (3) it means personal obedience to the word of Christ, an obedience that can be seen in daily life.

Another way to describe the filling of the Spirit, then, is to speak of being subject to the "control" of the Spirit, which means being subject to the "word of Christ." The contrast in Ephesians 5:18 between the filling of the Spirit and getting *drunk on wine* is understandable in terms of control. The contrast between drunkenness and being filled with the Spirit has perplexed many. Here also the context can come to our aid. Ephesians has just characterized the immorality known to its readers in terms of sexually immoral action and speech. Various New Testament passages focus on different sets of evil behavior, including drunkenness. For example, in Romans 13:13 several distinct sets of behavior are identified and listed, one of them being drunkenness: "Let us behave decently, as in the daytime, not in orgies and drunkenness, not in sexual immorality and debauchery, not in dissension and jealousy." Peter lists drunkenness as one of several sins that characterize pagans: "For you have spent enough time in the past doing what pagans choose to do—living in debauchery, lust, drunkenness, orgies, carousing and detestable idolatry" (1 Pet 4:3; compare Lk 21:34; 1 Cor 6:10; Gal 5:21). Thus Ephesians is introducing here another type of pagan sin it had not yet mentioned—drunkenness.

There is a sense in which drink "controls" a person. This is done not directly but by lowering inhibitions and letting the lower nature, the "flesh," perform in a way a sober person might not allow to be seen in public. This work of the flesh should be restrained and replaced by the filling of the Spirit (compare Gal 5:16-26).

Drunkenness is cited, therefore, both as a specific example of sinful behavior and as something that is—in its effect—the antithesis of being filled with the Spirit. If so, the allegation mentioned in Acts 2:13 that the disciples who were filled with the Spirit "had too much wine" is especially relevant. Surely drunkenness was not in that case thought of as an immoral state but as a temporary experience of exhilaration. But since Ephesians 5:18 specifically links drunkenness with *debauchery,* we can understand the filling of the Spirit and the associated celebratory activities in the following verses as the Christian antithesis to pagan revelry. It is worth noting that much pagan religious revelry involved immorality. These verses paint a picture, in contrast to pagan partying, of pure rejoicing and mutual encouragement.

While I was studying this verse we moved from a 1950s-type split-level house to a 1990s version of a ranch home (all on one level). Instead of four levels of small rooms we have a simplified, spacious living arrangement. Separate family and living rooms have been replaced by a "great room," modest in size but open to other rooms and enhanced by a cathedral ceiling. Once we were moved in, I hastily reassembled our stereo system (cables temporarily all over the place) and played one of my favorite organ and brass CDs. The music filled the great room and the entire house. It also filled me to the point that I was overwhelmed to tears by the magnificence and beauty of God's creation of music. As I prayed, I reflected on the fact that if one can be so filled and moved by the sensory experience of music, the effect of the filling of the Holy Spirit is completely, utterly and infinitely beyond that emotion.

The Need for Joyful Results (5:19-21) Because of the form of the Greek verbs in verses 19-21 (see the note below), they could express the result of the Spirit's filling, the circumstances in which it takes place or commands in connection with that filling. It is possible that Paul was not thinking of one sense to the exclusion of others. That is, he could be thinking of them as results that ought to take place, because they characterize the corporate life of truly Spirit-filled believers. The joy expressed in music and thanksgiving and the benefits of mutual submission, then, are results of the filling of the Spirit—but also what we need to experience in our life together.

Psalms, hymns and spiritual songs may refer to different kinds of religious music. *Psalms* could be from what we know as the book of Psalms, *hymns* could denote worship directed to God, and *spiritual songs* could be more spontaneous, possibly for mutual encouragement. However, it is often noted that these are not necessarily distinct from

---

5:21, 33 The word for *reverence* in verse 21 and the word for *respect* in verse 33 are both from Greek words for fearing. When the noun "fear," or the verb "to fear," occurs in the biblical text, it is sometimes difficult to know whether to modify it in translation. To use "fear" in a contemporary translation can evoke fright rather than reverence. Sometimes

each other in genre, but rather are overlapping if not synonymous terms. More significant than any difference between these is what they accomplish. (1) The singing is a kind of conversation among believers. Verse 19 begins with the word "speaking," which implies that the content of the songs is a communication with others. The dative form of *one another (heautois)* could indicate either that the communication is "to *one another*"(NIV) or "among yourselves" (NRSV). (2) The singing arises from the heart, implying both that it is sincere and that it is not merely superficially "joining in" a community song. (3) It is *to the Lord,* which fortifies the truly spiritual nature of the song—in contrast to the unholy conversation and coarse joking in the Ephesians' former state. (4) They are no longer idolatrous but are *giving thanks to God the Father.* (5) The words *always* and *for everything* are comprehensive and indicate a way of life, not just the experience of a moment. This amplifies the meaning of being filled with the Spirit. (6) Their thanksgiving is *in the name of our Lord Jesus Christ,* showing that they are now in the kingdom of Christ and of God (contrast v. 5) and that Christ has shone upon them (v. 14).

Submit in verse 21 is, like the verbs in verses 19-20, a participle ("submitting") and so grammatically appears in sequence with those verbs. Yet it also introduces a new subject, household relationships (5:22-33), and a new motive, *reverence for Christ.* The theme of *reverence* also appears in verse 33 *(the wife must respect her husband)* and 6:5 *(slaves, obey . . . with respect).*

The believer's attitude of reverence and respect to Christ should set the tone for the wife's reverence and respect for her husband. Apart from the exegesis of this term in each phrase (see note), this raises the matter of the rhetorical significance of these similar terms. The device of using similar words and phrases was often used to signal the beginning and end of a section. If it has that function here, verse 21 belongs with verses 22-33. Commentators and translators have failed to reach agreement on how to place this verse. It is perhaps best to see it as a transition verse. The phrase *wives, submit* in verse 22 actually lacks

---

that is exactly what it should do. Markus Barth thinks that is the case here, but his argument is that "Jesus Christ is to be feared because his 'love' is full of power and simply overwhelming" (Barth 1974b:667). That kind of fear is more like reverence than terror. An important Scripture on this matter is 1 John 4:18, "There is no fear in love."

that verb in a significant early papyrus and a significant early manuscript, but it is clear that the reader is mentally to supply that thought from *submit* in verse 21. Therefore verse 21 cannot be separated from verse 22 any more than it can be disjoined from verse 20.

There are two possible ways to view the mutual submission taught in verse 21. One is to see it in terms of classes (groups, roles or ranks), with one another meaning that members of one group submit to members of another group in one direction only, according to the group's function (as in military rank). The other interpretation is that it applies to interpersonal relationships among individuals, with each deferring at appropriate times to the other. This seems more in accord with the theme of verses 18-20, Spirit-filled believers ministering to one another.

If classes are in view, then, just as in the military, where those in a particular rank are always subject to those in a rank superior rank to theirs, certain groups (in this case, wives) would always be submissive—that is, obedient—to certain other groups (husbands). This would mean that in the following section (vv. 22-33) husbands are always in charge. But if individuals are in view, every believer should have an attitude of willing submission to others, rather than insisting on individual rights. Christian wives should be submissive, but husbands should not be drill sergeants.

One reason that some choose the submission-by-class interpretation is that the Greek word for submit (the passive of *hypotassō*) can require obedience in the appropriate context (again, the military being an example). This is lexically true. Yet we should observe that in the parallel sections about children and slaves, the word is not *submit* but "obey" (*hypakouō*, 6:1, 5). If the wife's submission were always in the form of obedience, Paul could have made that unambiguous by using "obey" in the introductory statement (5:22), instead of omitting the verb and letting the reader assume that it was the same verb as in the previous verse on mutual submission.

Another reason advanced for thinking that mutual submission is in terms of immutable role or rank relationships is that it is logically

_____

5:22 The ancient social codes regarding family relationships (and civil relationships as well) are sometimes known as "household codes." Scholars sometimes use the German term *Haustafeln*. Perhaps the best known of the early Greek philosophers who listed such

impossible for every individual in a group to be submissive to every other individual. This reason may seem logically true, that at any given moment it would be difficult to have complete mutual submission. But it loses its force when compared with Philippians 2:3, "Consider others better then yourselves." Certainly not every Christian is inferior to every other, but in humility one can *esteem* all others higher than oneself. Likewise it is possible on one occasion to defer to another, submitting to that person's will, with the situation being reversed at another time. There is nothing illogical about mutual submission.

Whether in the context of verses 18-20 or of verses 22-33, the idea of submitting is not on the surface as appealing as being joyful, but the result of this attitude can have a wonderful effect in the life of believers together. It has practical as well as spiritual benefits, as will be seen as the next section unfolds.

The Radical Change in Human Relationships (5:22—6:9) It is in the way we relate to one another that people should see the depth of God's work, and the effect of the Spirit's filling, in our lives. Some aspects of this have already appeared in 4:25—5:2. Verses 19-21 of chapter 5 speak of our relationship together in worship. Now Paul approaches the most intimate human relationship, marriage.

Christian Marriage (5:22-33) This is an extremely important and difficult passage for several reasons: (1) It pertains to the relationship that God established at the very beginning of human society (Gen 2:24; compare Eph 5:31). (2) That relationship is under great strain in contemporary society. (3) The roles of men and women, both in marriage and in general, have been the subject of much recent discussion.

The following questions are among those that have been raised concerning this passage:

□ Does it teach that women have a submissive role simply because of their sex?

□ Does the kind of submission taught here imply that women are inferior?

---

duties is Aristotle. These codes occur in various forms, and scholarly opinions about the evidence for a consistent tradition vary. The "code" Paul teaches here is uniquely Christian.

☐ Does the statement that the husband is the *head* of the wife mean that he has authority over her?

The following observations may help in addressing such questions.

The submission of wives (5:22-24). Since verse 22 is closely connected with verse 21, even taking its unexpressed verb from that verse (see the preceding discussion), the significance of mutual submission for family relationships must be reviewed carefully. It is sometimes pointed out that the three examples of husband and wife, children and parents, and slaves and masters demonstrate mutual submission. In a limited sense this is true. That is, a husband may give up his life for the sake of his wife as Christ did for his "bride"; a father may, for his children's good, give up his tendency to provoke them; and the master may give up the right to threaten his slave. Each is a form of submission, the yielding of one's assumed "rights."

The submission of a wife, along with that of children and slaves, is a pattern of relationship that is reminiscent of centuries of ancient social codes. Pagan philosophers had long been teaching such patterns (and others, such as civic roles) as proper behavior. So when Paul put the emphasis on the husband, the parent and the master, that much would have been familiar to those who knew this pattern. It was not news to wives that they should be submissive to their husbands. The "news" was that such submission now (1) was to be done for the sake of the Lord (v. 22) and (2) was balanced by the love of the husband even to the point of self-sacrifice (v. 25). It is striking that there is no command here for the husband to rule his wife. His only instruction is to love and care for her. The husband should not claim authority over his wife the way a Roman man used to. In that system, which underwent changes during the period of the early empire, a woman used to be under the *manus* ("hand") of her father and at marriage came under the control of her husband. Unfortunately, some Christian husbands have claimed authority, even to the extreme of abuse, in the name of "headship." In fact, however, such abusive behavior tends toward pagan rather than Christian moral standards.

Paul's teaching thus avoids an extreme view of male superiority, including the idea that wives must be submissive simply because they are women. Such a view was advocated in his day, for example, by the ancient Jewish historian Josephus, who taught that women were inferior and should be obedient (*Contra Apionem* 2.24.199). Yet Paul's instructions do support a household arrangement that would have been approved by many Hellenistic moral philosophers of his day. Because of this, some think his intent was to urge Christians to maintain order in their households such as would commend the new Christian faith to thoughtful pagans.

That is clearly the point regarding the submission of wives in 1 Peter 3:1-7. It is also consistent with Titus 2:5, where women are to be submissive to their husbands "so that no one will malign the grace of God." The fact that social acceptance of Christianity is the purpose in Titus 2 is clear from the other instructions, where young men are to be good examples "so that those who oppose you may be ashamed because they have nothing bad to say about us" (2:8) and where slaves should be subject to their masters "so that in every way they will make the teaching about God our Savior attractive" (2:10).

Therefore even though Ephesians makes no such reference to the reputation of Christian families among unbelievers (and though the parallel in Col 3:18—4:1 is also without any such explanatory comments), there is biblical reason to suppose that Paul may have had this in mind along with other purposes. Some even hold that since Paul in that social context provides governing rules for slaves and masters, and since this is a relationship neither we nor he would tolerate today, it is possible that Paul would not have been as strong today on the submission of wives. These, however, are matters of supposition.

As noted above, the manuscripts that are generally considered older and more accurate omit the word *submit* in verse 22. That does not mean this was not in Paul's mind, but that it was assumed from the previous verse. Therefore the instructions to wives in this context are not isolated but are linked to the call for mutual submission. This connection means that the submissive attitude described in verses 22-33 is a further expression of, and is enabled by, the filling of the Spirit in verse 18.

As to the Lord does not mean that the wife treats her husband as though he were the Lord, but rather that this submission is not an arbitrary capitulation to a husband's will but a means of honoring the Lord.

Whatever inferences may be drawn from the teaching on mutual submission, it clearly cannot mean a complete exchange of roles. As Christ and the church cannot exchange places, the analogy used does not permit husband and wife to exchange places either. And whatever social reasons there may have been for Paul's use of a household code, it still has a theological (specifically a christological) basis. The analogy Paul uses in verse 23 is that just as Christ is *head* of the church, so the husband is *head* of the wife.

The meaning of *head* in this context is therefore crucial. The word's meanings, as noted earlier, are not uniform. The Greek language did not assign as strong a leadership/authority meaning to *kephalē* as the Hebrew apparently did to *rōš and the Latin to caput.* Because of the strong connotation of *caput,* it was easy for the Latin church fathers to interpret *head* in this passage strongly. The most common word for "head" in Hebrew was *rōš* . When pre-Christian Jewish scholars translated the Old Testament into Greek (the Septuagint or LXX), they sometimes avoided the normal Greek word *kephalē* when the Hebrew *rōš* meant rule or authority (as in the word *leader)* and used instead a stronger synonym such as *archōn.* If *kephalē* had the unambiguous, univocal meaning of rule or authority, this would not have been necessary.

Such detail is important if we are to realize that Paul's use of *head* here is not harsh. In fact he will immediately nuance it with a reference to the husband's responsibility to the wife. But on the other hand, to exclude all sense of leadership from the word would be to ignore an important part of its history and use. It is true that it could mean "source" (and Eve did come from Adam, who was to care for her), and there is more evidence for this than some scholars have acknowledged. What is sometimes missed, though known by classical Greek scholars, is that the word *kephalē* had a more general figurative meaning of "prominence."

5:23 On the meaning of *kephalē* see also the comments on 1:22 and 4:15, and the note on the latter. Regarding the choice of a word other than *kephalē* in the LXX when the Hebrew term signifies authority, Klyne Snodgrass finds that out of 180 times when the idea of authority is present, *kephalē* was only used 16 times (Snodgrass 1996:295)!

5:25-27 There is a remarkable double literary background to the passage about husbands and wives. In addition to the secular codes recalled by verses 22-23, there is an Old Testament setting for verses 25-27, the relationship with Israel into which the Lord

While it is important to avoid "illegitimate totality transfer" (reading all possible meanings of a word into its usage in a single passage), it is also important not to limit the meaning by a predetermined choice. Whatever the main thrust of the word *head* as used here may be ("leadership," "caring," "prominence"), it certainly indicates a special responsibility for the husband that is parallel to the ministry of Christ to the church.

The fact that Christ is the *Savior* of the church does not mean that the husband necessarily has to "save" his wife in some way. But it does point out the special relationship Christ (the word *he* is emphatic) had to the church, which certainly added to his right to be its head.

The implications of submission become more explicit in verse 24. It is not to be selective, refused when inconvenient or distasteful, but comprehensive, *in everything*. A slightly different Greek phrase, though properly translated the same way ("in everything"), appears in the exhortation to children and slaves in Colossians 3:20, 22. But comprehensiveness is just what some wives fear. An unreasonable husband, an abuser, one who is sexually demanding, can use this verse wrongly as a club to gain his way. The ideal is a wife who is not withholding submission selfishly and a husband who does not demand it unreasonably.

The caring love of Christ as a model for husbands (5:25-27). In telling husbands to love their wives, Paul goes beyond the familiar Greco-Roman codes. It is significant that he does not use the words that would have been expected in that society, "Husbands, rule your wives," in contrast to the exhortation about wives' submission. This can easily be missed, but it is crucial. What this does is to express a way in which a husband, for the sake of his wife, can also express submission: forgoing his own comfort and safety to the point of death.

(Yahweh) entered as a husband to a wife. Ezekiel 16:1-14 is one of several passages employing this imagery, and verses 9-14 in particular use descriptive terminology about washing and adorning that probably lies behind Ephesians 5:25-27. The love songs in the Song of Songs, where the bride is cherished as the Beloved, also celebrate the beauty of a bride (as in Eph 1:8; 4:1; 5:9; 6:1). See Sampley 1971. Verses 25-27 therefore owe a great deal to the Old Testament for their beautiful poetic imagery and form.

So the parallel between the submission of wives and that of the church finds correspondence in the parallel between the love of husbands and that of Christ, both expressed in giving oneself up for the beloved.

The truth that Christ *gave himself up for* the church elevates the love of the husband far above mere social convention or emotional feeling. A husband who may at times feel he has some right to dominate his wife cannot justify any action that preserves his life, well-being and sense of personal fulfillment at the expense of his wife's. The heart of the gospel and of Christianity is the sacrifice of Christ in our place. The substitutionary atonement of Christ was accomplished once for all on the cross (Heb 9:28). No one can repeat that saving action, but we may follow Jesus' model of self-sacrifice, giving up our physical life for the sake of another. The reference to the sacrifice of Christ shows the extent of his love, so that husbands will not have a lower standard, but also suggests that a husband should stand ready actually to repeat such self-sacrifice, if necessary, for the sake of his wife.

Verses 26-27 show the purpose for which Christ gave himself for the church. There are two purpose clauses: (1) *to make her holy* and (2) *to present her to himself as a radiant church*. Holiness, or sanctification, is linked with a specific *washing,* the nature of which is not completely clear. The use of the article *(the washing)* suggests something the readers knew of. Some commentators refer to an allegory in Ezekiel 16:1-22 that describes a neglected baby from whom the blood of the birth process has not been washed. The baby grows and (in a telescoped sequence) is washed and married, only to become a prostitute. Parts of this marital allegory of grace may be applicable. Otherwise Ephesians could simply refer to the Jewish custom of a bridal washing. Also some New Testament passages about salvation include references to water, such as John 3:5 and Titus 3:5.

5:26 The image of a resplendent bride recalls two passages in the book of Revelation. These illustrate the importance in the first century of bridal apparel, although they do not refer to the present passage. One is Revelation 19:7-8: " 'Let us rejoice and be glad and give him glory! For the wedding of the Lamb has come, and his bride has made herself ready. Fine linen, bright and clean, was given her to wear.' (Fine linen stands for the

One of the reasons for unity in the church mentioned in Ephesians 4:5 was baptism. Although baptism is not connected with washing in most New Testament references (in contrast with other religions, whose rites of water symbolized cleansing from sin), it is so connected in Acts 22:16: "Get up, be baptized and wash your sins away, calling on his name." If that is the case here, *the word* could be the baptismal formula (usually concluding with "In the name of the Father and of the Son and of the Holy Spirit") or perhaps a message given at that time. The position of *through* (or "by") *the word* at the end of the phrase shows that the effective agent in the *cleansing* is not water but the word itself.

The perspective on salvation that is emphasized in chapter 2 of Ephesians is that salvation is not only for our benefit but also for God's. We are reconciled to God and to one another. Happy as we are over God's blessing, we may forget that through the cross God has won us for himself. Peter expressed this in 1 Peter 3:18: "For Christ died for sins once for all, the righteous for the unrighteous, to bring you to God." In Ephesians 5 the image is of a groom who presents the bride to himself. Christ does not need someone to "give away the bride." He is both groom and Lord.

In this presentation the bride appears in all the beauty Christ has given her. The picture is both artistic and theological. The bride appears in all her youthful attractiveness ("without a spot or wrinkle," NRSV) and morally pure (*holy and blameless;* compare 1:4; Phil 2:15; Heb 9:14, among other passages).

This description of what Christ has done for the church goes beyond what a husband can do, for only Christ can make his bride pure. But a husband can certainly help his wife be radiant by his attitude toward her. If one dominates his wife, suppressing her God-given abilities and spontaneity, he is obscuring the radiance of her person. Too often a Christian woman's vitality, her ebullient spirit, is obscured by a covering of supposedly spiritual meekness superimposed by her husband, and her personal and spiritual gifts never find full development or expression.

---

righteous acts of the saints.)" That passage is referring to a future event, as is Revelation 21:2: "I saw the Holy City, the new Jerusalem, coming down out of heaven from God, prepared as a bride beautifully dressed for her husband." The Ephesians passage describes the *present* relationship between Christ and his bride as a model for husbands and wives. For a strong argument in support of this position see Lincoln 1990:377.

Further reasons for a husband's love (5:28-32). Those who provide premarital and marital counseling often hear couples express deficient ideas of love. When asked what they mean by "I love you," one or the other is likely to answer in self-centered language about *being* loved, feeling good, enjoying the other's personality and so on. But here in Ephesians the dominant idea is *giving* oneself for the good of the other. Even Christ's presentation of the bride to himself means her enhancement. So as Paul proceeds to the next thoughts in verse 28, he refers back to the example of Christ with the words *in this way (houtōs)*.

It may seem strange that husbands are to love their wives *as their own bodies.* That can only be understood in the light of the remarkable union between husband and wife, which (1) is modeled on the caring relationship of Christ to the church, (2) was established at creation (v. 31) and (3) is reintroduced (v. 32) in a mystical way in terms of Christ and the church.

There is no mystical confusion between the body of the husband and that of the wife, as the language might be misunderstood to mean. The comparison with Christ and the church rules that out. Rather, verse 28 expresses the quality of the husband's love and the extent to which he is to care for his wife. It may seem as though the wife is demeaned by the reference to the husband's feeding and caring for his body as an analogy of his caring for her. That is not so for two reasons. First, this is simply a realistic statement of the way a man normally cares for himself, an attitude of caring that should be given equally to his wife. Second, in the culture of Paul's day brides were usually teenage girls, who would not have the status—to say nothing of income—of most brides today. They were therefore dependent on their husbands.

Beyond that, however, is the "one flesh" relationship to which verse 31 refers, quoting Genesis 2:24. This is foundational to the teaching in this section. Following the teaching of Jesus when he was asked about

---

5:31 Interpretations of Genesis 2:24 and Ephesians 5:31-32 in Jewish, Gnostic and Christian writings are numerous, varied and often bewildering. Among the many comments and bibliographies on these that are accessible in the scholarly literature and reference works, two commentaries on Ephesians provide good source materials: Barth 1974b:720-38 and Lincoln 1990:382-83.

5:32 On the use of the word *mystery,* see Ephesians 1:9; 3:3, 4, 6, 9; 6:19, and comments.

divorce (Mt 19:5), Paul goes all the way back to creation for his basis. Throughout the millennia of biblical history this truth endures. It is especially striking against the background of a patriarchal society, when the wife could be absorbed into her husband's household. The husband must deliberately recognize the new entity of marriage by stepping out of his former family unit and forming a new one with his wife alone. This may not seem as important today, when so many families are already fragmented, but in another sense it is all the more important, in that there are unseen emotional ties not only between the husband and his parents but between also the wife and her parents (as well as with siblings and others). These relationships can easily intrude on a marriage to the point where the unseen presence of a mother- or father-in-law can be almost as influential as if the parent were really there. While "one flesh" brings the physical, sexual relationship immediately to mind, it extends to the whole new relationship formed between spouses.

The use of the word *mystery* at this point could be taken merely as a reference to something mysterious. It is related, however, to its uses elsewhere in Scripture, meaning both that which the human mind cannot know without divine revelation and that which God is doing in his wise plan. Paul understands through divine inspiration that the teaching of Genesis on marriage is neither solely physical or social nor allegorical or mystical, as some Jewish and Gnostic thinkers held. Rather, Paul affirms (using the emphatic *egō* for *I*) that the proper understanding of the relationship between husband and wife is that it is an exposition of the relationship between Christ and the church.

Returning to the individual instructions to husband and wife, Paul addresses *each one of you* and summarizes their individual responsibilities, the husband to *love his wife as himself* and the wife to *respect her husband*. (See comments also on 5:21 and 5:33 regarding *respect*.) This of course does not exclude love on the wife's part nor respect on the

---

As the language of the ancient church changed from Greek to Latin, the Latin *sacramentum* was used for the Greek *mystērion*. That meant the introduction of ideas from *sacramentum* that did not correspond exactly to the use of *mystērion* in this passage and elsewhere. *Sacramentum* came to be used for a sign that points to a divine reality; baptism is one example. For this reason and others the Roman Catholic Church developed a concept of marriage as a "sacrament."

husband's. Both need emphasis again today.

Fathers and Children (6:1-4) Parents sometimes use this passage as a club to bring their children into submission. Since it is Scripture, and specifically a quotation from the Ten Commandments, it is indeed authoritative. But parents can go beyond requiring appropriate obedience and vent their own frustrations and anger on their children. Abuse can be verbal as well as physical. It is possible for a father to believe that he is pleasing God by observing Ephesians 4:26 by not being angry with other adults, while he acts in such a way as to cause anger in his children, justifying his actions by referring to 6:1.

Fathers in ancient Rome had extraordinary power over their children. In the Greco-Roman tradition, unwanted children, especially girls, were exposed to the elements or otherwise disposed of. Abortion was also practiced. But Christian parents, Paul says, must not act as though their children were their possession. A father who rightly refuses to allow a child to dominate the family's selection of TV programs may overstep by refusing to allow a teenager his or her rightful role in choosing a college. Also, just as husbands, in the spirit of mutual submission (v. 21), are to care for their wives, even to the point of self-sacrifice (5:25-30), and as masters are to restrain themselves from threatening their slaves (6:9), so fathers are to moderate their attitudes to their children (6:4).

As in the lists known as "household codes" in the ancient world, children are to obey, and this passage states that this is *right*. But as with Christian husbands and wives and Christian slaves and masters, there is a Christian dimension to the duties of Christian *children*. Therefore as 5:22 instructs wives and 6:5 instructs slaves that when they submit and obey respectively, they should do this as to the Lord, so should children. The command in verses 1-3 about children's obedience is given not to fathers but to the children themselves. The implication is that children should learn to obey rather than their fathers forcing obedience. Children are people, to be respected and acknowledged as responsible, though young; and they are part of the Christian family. One way to tell the

---

6:1 The manuscript evidence for the phrase *in the Lord* is uncertain. It is lacking in some significant manuscripts, and it could be argued that some copyist found the text without the words and tried to bring this passage in line with 5:22 and 6:5 by inserting the

heart of a pastor is to note whether he speaks only to adults or whether he relates well to children also.

The command to children is strong, but it is not harsh. On the contrary, the law, and now Paul, provides a wonderful motivation in two parts: (1) *that it may go well with you* and (2) *that you may enjoy long life on the earth.* In Deuteronomy 5:6-21, the second, third and fourth commandments are supported with reasons, but this is the first and only one (within the Decalogue itself) that is accompanied by a promise.

The first part of the motivation, well-being, is easy to appropriate from the Old Testament and apply to children in the Christian family. The second part, *long life on the earth,* presents obvious difficulties. Originally this referred to continuance of God's people in the land of Israel. But can it be changed to mean a long earthly life? What about good children who die young? It may help to keep in mind Psalm 103:3: the Lord "heals all your diseases." Some believers are not healed; otherwise none would ever die. But it is still true that God is the Healer; the healing of all diseases comes ultimately from him, and some live longer than they otherwise would because they trust God. So some children may die young, victims (as we all are) of death and sin in the world, but there are many ways in which God blesses obedient children with a good life.

The word to fathers does not negate or soften the preceding word to children, but it does put a heavy responsibility on the parent. One of the perversions of our sinful human nature is the tendency to provoke someone else to do something in front of others that we are feeling or doing inwardly ourselves. So a father can feel hostility to a disobedient child and prod that child to be the one to express hostility outwardly. To realize this subtle influence on the child may help us to understand why the text uses the strong Greek adversative *alla* ("but, on the contrary") when introducing the next clause (NIV *instead*). The opposite of inciting children to react is inspiring them to learn.

It was typical in ancient education for the mother to teach young

---

phrase. Nevertheless, it is present in p[46], Sinaiticus, Alexandrinus and others. While doubtful, it is included for the purpose of this commentary.

children but when they reached what we would call "school age," or a little older, for the father to continue their education. The word *paideia,* translated *training* in the NIV, had a distinguished significance in the Greco-Roman world. More than teaching and learning facts, it was the formation of the person, which involved discipline. The other word, *instruction,* could (though not necessarily) encompass the element of admonishing someone. Together these terms convey the sober responsibility of a father to see to the development of his children into personal and spiritual (note the words *of the Lord*) maturity.

Slaves and Masters (6:5-9) In the nineteenth century Christians as well as others debated slavery. In the course of the debate, one side made strong use of the biblical passages in which slavery is assumed. Paul did not urge or personally work toward the freeing of slaves or the dissolution of the practice. This fact was wrongly (as we see it now) taken to indicate tacit approval on Paul's part. Given the depth to which slavery was embedded in ancient society and the disastrous results that occurred when attempts were made to overthrow the system, we know that there was little Paul could have done. He made good progress toward alleviating the stresses of slavery by his teaching in this passage.

There are some similarities between the instructions to slaves and those to women. Both are told to have *respect,* for their master (6:5) and husband (5:33) respectively, as Christians are to have for Christ when submitting to one another (5:21). The word for respect also can mean "fear" (see comments on 5:21, 33), but the NIV reserves that translation for the second Greek noun here in 6:5, *tromos* (which can include trembling, the translation it receives in the NRSV). Given the ideas of *fear, respect* and trembling that are contained in these two Greek words, the reader can grasp how important it was that Christian slaves were not to despise their owners as many others did.

If that was true within the environment of slavery, Christians in a free society must be careful to both have and show respect for those whose

---

6:5 In reading Swartley 1983 one is brought to realize that there is some similarity between the hermeneutical methods used to justify slavery in the nineteenth century and to restrict women's ministry today. That does not settle either issue, but does suggest caution in drawing conclusions on any issue too quickly from individual passages.

6:9 I encourage readers to consult encyclopedia articles and other works on slaves in

actions may not be commendable. Disrespect for parents, employers, spouses and government officials is not appropriate for a Christian. Such disrespect can be communicated not only through outright criticism (which actually can be offered directly to the person in a respectful way) but also through attitude and jokes.

The next term, *sincerity of heart,* leads to the following verse (v. 6), which urges a consistency of service even when the slaves are not under watch. At the end of verse 5 Paul adds to *respect, fear* and *sincerity* the words *just as you would obey Christ.* This picks up the previously noted *out of reverence for Christ* (5:21), *as to the Lord* (5:22) and, if the words are in the original (see note), *in the Lord* (6:1). In turn this is reflected in the phrase *like slaves of Christ* in verse 6. Verse 7 further emphasizes the importance of this attitude both in the word *wholeheartedly,* which overlaps *sincerity* in meaning, and in the participial phrase *as if you were serving [literally, "as to"] the Lord, not men.* This is a remarkable series of exhortations, clearly intended not to keep slaves "in their place" but to encourage them to have a positive Christian attitude. Support for this attitude comes from the assurance that God will *reward* everyone who does *good,* whether as a slave or as a free person.

As in the previous examples of human relationships, there should be reciprocity. Not only should Christian masters refrain from threatening, but they should recognize their equality with slaves before the One who is the *Master* of both. Whether or not one considers the self-restraint of husband, father and master as a form of mutual submission, the instructions in this Christian "household code" were remarkable for that age.

☐ The Spiritual Battle (6:10-20)

Without doubt one of the most uneasy areas of the Christian life is what we call the spiritual battle. It is uneasy because of the fearful threat of the devil, who cruises the earth looking for victims: "Be self-controlled

---

the ancient world. For some years a book by W. L. Westermann, the esteemed ancient historian and expert on ancient slavery (1964), has been a major reference work on the subject. For an important study on slavery with respect to 1 Corinthians 7:21, see Bartchy 1973.

and alert. Your enemy the devil prowls around like a roaring lion looking for someone to devour" (1 Pet 5:8). Our "ancient foe" has been a threat since Eve "was deceived by the serpent's cunning," and he remains active (2 Cor 11:3). He had access to the heavenly council and sought to discredit God by attacking Job (Job 1:6-12). Satan not only tempts individuals but also influences nations (Dan 10:13, 20-21; Rev 20:1-3). This is complicated by the believer's repeated problems with his or her own temptations. Are these temptations caused, intensified or used by Satan, or are temptations independent of Satan's activities? We know from James 1:13-15 that God does not tempt us. James does not say, however, that temptation comes instead from Satan; rather it comes from our own "evil desire." Another passage in Ephesians, 4:26-27, does tell us that the devil can employ a human situation, in this instance anger, to gain a "foothold."

People in the ancient world were fearful of a variety of influences. In earlier days the Greeks feared the anger of their gods. Then, as belief in the traditional pantheon of gods waned, there was a dread of fate, and then an apprehension of mere chance. Astrology developed largely as a way to chart one's course in an uncertain environment. Jewish people, on the other hand, knew all too well the damaging effect of pagan gods on their ancestors. Today opposition to Christianity takes various forms, among them New Age ideas, occultism, secular humanism and postmodernism. Some think supernatural forces stand behind these.

But given many expressions of evil, how much is due to the direct activity of a personal devil and how much is of human origin? Some Christians are prone to blame lack of control over habits—smoking, for example—on Satan rather than on our sinful nature or lack of self-discipline. As with the matter of temptation, it is presumptuous to attribute more activities to Satan than Scripture does.

Yet where it *is* possible to discern satanic influence, how does one fight against such a supernatural force? Again, various methods are used, including vocal confrontation, prayer, twelve-step support groups and various practices to nurture spiritual growth. Sometimes demonstrations

---

6:10-20 Clinton E. Arnold (1989) offers convincing evidence that fear of supernatural powers and the use of magic against them were common in Ephesus. He deals with a number of passages in Ephesians that he thinks are relevant to this background. His chapter

in front of abortion clinics, boycotting the products of an advertiser who supports sex and violence on TV, and campaigning against political candidates because of their vote on certain issues are thought of as storming the bastions of Satan. What does Ephesians have to say about this? Does the statement that "our struggle is not against flesh and blood" have any bearing on it?

It is important to understand that Satan is not directly active in everything evil; he is not omnipresent. But where there is satanic influence, no method of resistance can possibly "work" that is not grounded on a biblical understanding of spiritual warfare. That is an immense topic, but the major source of information is the passage before us. Therefore this passage in Ephesians is of urgent importance for all believers and is preliminary to any conclusions about the victorious Christian life.

It is assumed here, as was taught in Ephesians 1:20-23, that Christ himself has gained ultimate victory over all hostile powers in the universe. That means that Paul's instructions about the spiritual battle are not given as a means by which we gain that ultimate victory. That belongs to Christ himself. But if that victory meant we are automatically destined to win every skirmish, there would be no need of teaching about the battle and the armor. Clearly we must apply the result of Christ's victory in our own lives. The victory of Christ in the supernatural arena must be achieved in our personal lives on earth.

The Importance of the Spiritual Battle (6:10-12) The word *finally* may seem strange at this point, since it is not a natural transition from the preceding household code. But it functions to call the readers to action in a way that is fitting in view of the whole practical section that began with 4:1, and in view of the entire teaching of Ephesians. There are some allusions to foregoing themes, but beyond these this section unveils to the reader the reality of an ongoing spiritual warfare that lies behind human spiritual and moral decisions.

The specific exhortation in this concluding section—the *peroratio,* as

---

"The Conflict with the Powers" (pp. 103-22) addresses 6:10-20 in particular. In a second work (1992) Arnold expands his study to deal with all the Pauline letters as they address the reality of evil powers.

the ancient stylists called such a persuasive appeal at the conclusion of an epistle—is to be *strong*. Paul's comments on strength are in four categories: (1) the exhortation to strength, (2) the source or means of strength, (3) the need for strength and (4) the employment of this strength.

1. The exhortation comes through clearly in the first sentence of the section. It would be possible for readers to be uplifted and challenged by the epistle thus far without realizing that their response is not a simple matter of appreciation and compliance. It is not that there have been no exhortations, but they have not yet been set in the context of the fierce unseen battle that requires superhuman strength.

The verb *be strong* implies a growing strength. This recalls Abraham's faith, whereby he did not waver in unbelief at the staggering promise of a child in his old age but "was strengthened in his faith and gave glory to God" (Rom 4:20). In 2 Timothy 2:1 Paul urges Timothy to be strong. Concepts in 1 Corinthians 16:13 are reminiscent of several ideas found also in our Ephesians passage: "Be on your guard" (compare Eph 6:18, *be alert*); "stand firm in the faith" (Eph 6:13-14); "be strong" (the Greek verb here is a cognate of the word *mighty* in *his mighty power,* Eph 6:10).

An interesting variation occurs in 1 John 2:14, "I write to you, young men, because you are strong . . . and you have overcome the evil one." What Paul urges in Ephesians is expressed in 1 John as already accomplished: they *are* strong and *have* overcome the evil one. It is doubtful that one general group of Christians, and those called "young" at that, would have somehow already accomplished what the readers of Ephesians are only now being introduced to. We may therefore propose that there is a sense in which all believers are victors on the basis of the victory Christ achieved in the cross, resurrection and ascension (compare Eph 1:20-23); yet we can at any time meet the enemy, and he—not by superior status or force but by deceit (6:11)—can cause us to fall.

6:10 The reason the NRSV and some other translations have a longer phrase here (such as "strength of his power" rather than *mighty power*) is because they choose to render the use of the Greek genitive literally. The NIV chooses to render the Greek idiom in a way that shows that one word characterizes the other.

2. The source of this strength is the Lord himself, and in particular the *mighty power* just referred to (v. 10). The means are the various pieces of armor, not only as separate parts but as a whole, *the full armor* (v. 11). While this phrase represents a single Greek word, *panoplia*, that word is itself a compound of two words: all or whole + tool or weapon. Its common meaning is "the full equipment of the heavily armored foot-soldier." The English term that is derived from this, *panoply*, can refer to full protective covering, ceremonial dress or a complete display of something in all its parts. In this case the emphasis seems to be not so much on being in full military dress or having every weapon as on having total protection, with enough of the individual pieces identified to show the need of God's full provision for the spiritual battle.

The effectiveness of ancient armor depended not only on the resistance of the individual sections to various types of weaponry but also on the extent to which the combined pieces covered the vital parts of the body. One reason Christians have sometimes found one or another method of spiritual warfare deficient is that the method we choose may be effective in some areas of spiritual battle but not comprehensive enough to protect us against all areas of temptation and attack.

3. There is a need for strength because of the existence of a vicious supernatural enemy. Verse 11 concludes with a warning against *the devil's schemes*. The phrase brings together the dark figure behind the caution in 4:27, "do not give the devil a foothold," and the reference to "scheming" in 4:14. Whereas the "scheming" in chapter 4 is the product of cunning, crafty people, here in chapter 6 it is directly attributed to the devil.

Verse 12 provides further reason for being strong and deploying the armor of God and goes on to name other supernatural enemies, using some of the same terminology found in 1:21 and 3:10 (see comments there). Unfortunately, throughout its history the Christian church has often tended to view human opponents as the enemy to be fought.

6:11 See Oepke 1954:295-302 for the varied uses of the term *panoplia*. Barth (1974b:761, 793-95) proposes the term "splendid armor," in part because, given that not every piece is mentioned, "whole armor" is inaccurate. However, "splendid armor" implies that the appearance is more significant than the function.

Sometimes this has been an exegetical position, concluding that structures of government constitute the enemy. Sometimes it has been de facto, as Christians lash out against those who oppose them. Paul's negative clarification *(not against)* should have prevented that error. The enemy is not a visible and relatively weak humanity (the meaning of *flesh and blood*), not even powerful human authorities. This enemy is in the heavenly realms and is therefore unseen, possessing a tactical advantage over those whose vision is earthbound.

In spite of the power of the enemy, however, Christians are not at a disadvantage. This epistle has repeatedly assured believers that they have both a perspective and a source of life and power that are supreme in the same heavenly realms (1:3, 10; 2:6; as well as 1:20; 3:10).

The list of opposing powers in 6:12 is a comprehensive one that overlaps those listed earlier. The different designations here are not separated by conjunctions. That is, rather than "the rulers . . . *and* the authorities . . . *and* the powers of this dark world," they are simply listed in sequence: *against the rulers, against the authorities, against the powers of this dark world, against the spiritual forces of evil in the heavenly realms* (NIV inserts an unwarranted *and* between the last two groups). This could allow the inference that these are different ways of describing the same general group of supernatural enemies. On the other hand it could be that different groups are indicated, with the omission of connectives being for the rhetorical purpose of staccato emphasis.

If there are distinct groups, are the powers ranked? Are levels of authority indicated by the order in this passage? *Rulers* and *authorities* were mentioned in the earlier lists in Ephesians, where they are not named as evil but are neutral. Here they certainly are evil. The very words indicate a superior rank, but whether this is a superiority over humanity or over other supernatural beings is not specified.

Scholars are generally in agreement that the next term, *kosmokratōr,*

6:12 *Flesh and blood* is a Semitic idiom (expressed in the Greek of this passage in reverse order, "blood and flesh"). It is used in a figurative way in several other New Testament passages. In Matthew 16:17 the revelation of the true identity of Jesus did not come to Peter from mere humanity but from the heavenly Father. First Corinthians 15:50 says that "flesh and blood cannot inherit the kingdom of God," in a context of teaching that what is perishable must be transformed into the imperishable. Paul did not consult with human beings ("flesh and blood") but received his revelation from God (Gal 1:16).

translated *the powers of this dark world*, has roots in astrological thought, in which this world was considered to be under the influence of the planets, which themselves represented personal forces. As time went on the term was used for a broad spectrum of power figures, from the Roman emperor (specifically Caracella) to pagan gods. It was not a designation of just one such god; in pagan syncretism the gods and their names were sometimes blended. Therefore the fact that one god, Serapis, was called by the term *kosmokratōr* does not restrict it to him. (His name is a composite of those of two gods, Osiris and Apis.) The fact that magical arts were practiced at Ephesus along with the customary pagan worship (Acts 19:23-34) prepares us for Paul's mention here of major supernatural forces behind such activities.

The last term Paul uses, *the spiritual forces of evil*, could be a summary expression for all such forces that exist. This is a sobering passage. We know Paul held that there were actual demons behind pagan gods (1 Cor 10:20-22). We know also that Satan deceives the nations (Rev 20:3). Given these realities, it would be not only wrong but foolish and dangerous to live the Christian life without being prepared for spiritual warfare.

While it may be difficult to identify and distinguish between the specific powers named here, the point is clearly made that whatever supernatural forces there may be in this universe, Christ has gained victory over them and so may we. To recognize that is not to diminish the immense spiritual force they represent. Were that the case, there would be no need for the armor and there would be no occasion for the battle.

4. Regarding the employment of this strength, the verb *stand* occurs in several places in the passage. In this introductory section it is a goal (*so that you can take your stand*, v. 11), as it is in verse 13 (*so that . . . you may be able to stand*). In verses 14-16 it is the main command (*Stand*

The actual beings Paul had in mind as our supernatural enemies, along with the whole reality of spiritual warfare, have often been researched and discussed. Among the most recent discussions (from different viewpoints) are Arnold 1989:64-68, Lincoln 1990:443-45 and Schnackenburg 1991:273-74. These writings contain references to primary source materials that range from Gnostic writings to Jewish writings of the Second Temple period, including the Dead Sea Scrolls, to the magical papyri, astrological writings and historical sources.

firm then). This may give the impression that the Christian has no further investment in the outcome of the spiritual war than to remain stationary.

Our problem is that we naturally interpret Paul's image in terms of contemporary warfare. The destructive weapons now available are used to penetrate far beyond any single line of defense, and defensive forces are not content to "hold the line" but must destroy the aggressor's ability to wage further warfare. But in the ancient form of hand-to-hand combat described here, the first duty of a line of soldiers standing side by side against attackers—often with large rectangular shields (as here) close to each other—was to prevent an incursion against the enemy's ultimate target.

In Christian warfare, Christ and his kingdom are that ultimate target. We are not called to perform individual heroics but to resist and prevail against Satan's attack on the kingdom of God. Christ won the victory when, in the power of the Spirit, he cast out demons. In the context of Matthew 12:22-32 Jesus is accused of driving out demons in the name of Beelzebub, a name for the evil one. But Jesus proclaimed that he was bringing the power of the kingdom against Satan (see especially v. 28). And in Luke 10, when the disciples reported that the demons were subject to them, Jesus replied, "I saw Satan fall like lightning from heaven" (v. 18). Also the death of Christ accomplished a key victory against Satan. "Since the children have flesh and blood, he too shared in their humanity so that by his death he might destroy him who holds the power of death—that is, the devil" (Heb 2:14). Further, we have already observed the victory of Christ in his ascension (Eph 1:20-23).

There is no need, then, for Christians to accomplish what has already been done. Instead we must resist the attempts of Satan both to retake territory no longer his and to defame Christ and his kingdom by causing us to fail. To *stand* is neither static nor passive, but the active accomplishment of our present task.

The Armor Needed for the Spiritual Battle (6:13-17) Since it is often a long step from theory to practice, transition words between the two in Scripture are especially important. We saw that the information given in verse 12 about the unseen powers is the reason for taking God's armor. That verse began with the word *for.* Now verse 13 looks back to verse 12 with the word *therefore* (Greek "on account of this"), and verse 14 continues the sequence with *then* (Greek "therefore"). This strong interconnection emphasizes the importance of taking the hostile powers seriously.

The content of verse 13 is essentially the same as that of the previous verses, with the addition of a reference to a *day* that is designated as *evil*. It sounds as though that day was not yet present, somewhat like the Old Testament phrase "the day of the Lord." This is a day, either imminent or in the "eschaton" (that is, a significant time of God's acts at the conclusion of history), when God acts decisively. But if *the day of evil* in verse 13 does not allude to a time the original readers were experiencing themselves, why would the passage give the impression that readers (then and now) should take up spiritual armor right away?

Since the writer refers to pieces of armor used by soldiers of that day, it would be natural to interpret the passage mainly on the basis of the military significance of each piece. While that would be instructive, the more important point of reference is the Old Testament book of Isaiah. There the various pieces are part of the armor of God himself, actually aspects of his own character.

But with righteousness he will judge the needy,
   with justice he will give decisions for the poor of the earth.
He will strike the earth with the rod of his mouth;
   with the breath of his lips he will slay the wicked.
Righteousness will be his belt
   and faithfulness the sash around his waist. (Is 11:4-5)
He put on righteousness as his breastplate,
   and the helmet of salvation on his head;
he put on the garments of vengeance
   and wrapped himself in zeal as in a cloak. (Is 59:17)
How beautiful on the mountains
   are the feet of those who bring good news,
who proclaim peace,
   who bring good tidings,
   who proclaim salvation,
who say to Zion,
   "Your God reigns!" (Is 52:7)

(The last passage here is not about warfare, but it probably lies behind verse 15 in the Ephesians passage.)

A survey of these passages, especially those in Isaiah 11 and 59, suggests that the significance of the armor is not as much in the individual pieces, important as they are, as in what they signify together as God's armor, which is also that of his Messiah. God revealed himself in the Old Testament as a warrior: "The LORD is a warrior; the LORD is his name" (Ex 15:3). But the passages in Isaiah have a more specific focus. The context of Isaiah 11:4-5 is clearly messianic:

A shoot will come up from the stump of Jesse;

from his roots a Branch will bear fruit. (v. 1)

The wolf will live with the lamb,

the leopard will lie down with the goat,

the calf and the lion and the yearling together;

and a little child will lead them . . . (v. 6; see also vv. 7-9)

Verses 3-4 predict that the Messiah will be concerned for justice and righteousness, followed by verse 5, which contains the reference to the belt of righteousness and the sash of faithfulness.

In Isaiah 59 the background is a lack of justice. God is able to hear and save his people, but they have alienated themselves from him by their sins (vv. 1-3). Further, there is a lack of justice (vv. 4, 8-9, 14-15), righteousness (vv. 9, 14) and truth (vv. 14-15). Therefore God moves into the situation wearing "righteousness as his breastplate" and "salvation" as his "helmet" to deal with his enemies. The passage concludes with a messianic promise:

"The Redeemer will come to Zion,

to those in Jacob who repent of their sins,"

declares the LORD. (v. 20)

As for the verse about the beautiful feet of "those who bring good news" (Is 52:7), this occurs in the section that immediately precedes the famous passage of Isaiah 52:13—53:12, which describes the Messiah as a suffering servant.

Therefore the armor of Ephesians is the armor of God and of his

---

6:15 Where the NIV has *the readiness that comes from* . . . the NRSV has "make you ready to proclaim . . ." The former understands the genitive *tou evangeliou* as source; the

Messiah, and the basic concerns are for (1) the achievement of right-eousness and justice and (2) the proclamation of God's truth that brings peace. It would seem appropriate to conclude as well that in Ephesians the point is not merely protection of God's people during satanic attack but the achievement of truth, righteousness and justice as well as of the peace brought by the gospel. We should not be so preoccupied with our personal spiritual struggles, obsessed with the possibility of satanic attack, that we neglect larger fields of conflict involving God's righteous-ness in this world.

The specific functions of the individual pieces of armor are fairly self-evident. Ancient warriors, like other people of the time, wore loose-fitting clothing. When approaching some task, athletic event or battle, they needed to gather this clothing together to permit freer movement. It was done in different ways for different purposes. (See 2 Kings 4:29; Job 38:3; Lk 12:35; Jn 13:4; and the figurative image in 1 Pet 1:13. The translations do not always convey the image of "binding" or "girding.") Preparation for action could entail the wearing of a foundational piece, perhaps of leather or an exterior belt or sash, or it could be just the gathering of loose folds. The Christian soldier wears the belt of *truth,* perhaps here as the first item put on under the others, because integrity of character is so impor-tant. That assumes that the truth specified here and in the background text of Isaiah is not so much verbal truth as truthfulness, or, as in the Old Testament, faithfulness.

The *breastplate* covered the major organs much as a bullet-proof vest does today. The moral quality of *righteousness* that characterized God in the Isaiah passages, that justice which is prized so highly in the prophets (for example, "What does the LORD require of you? To act justly and to love mercy and to walk humbly with your God," Micah 6:8), is essential for the one who must stand against evil.

It is interesting that although one might expect soldier's boots to be at the end of the list of equipment, that part of the equipment comes in the middle of Paul's list. This may be because of its importance for

latter may understand it as a genitive of reference, interpolating the words "to proclaim."

fulfilling the command to *stand*. *With your feet fitted* probably referred to *caligae* (from which the nickname of Emperor Caligula came), tough but light sandals (in the sense that the toes were open) that went partly up the leg, with soles studded with nails for a secure grip on the ground. Soldiers could wear them in hand-to-hand combat, rather than the heavy boots used in long marches. The purpose could be twofold: to maintain a solid footing, as commanded, and to be ready for action.

In Isaiah 52:7, and in Romans 10:15 where Isaiah is quoted, the emphasis is on the feet of the persons who announce *good news*. Lincoln (1990:448) observes that Ephesians follows Isaiah in referring to the *feet* being shod rather than to the actual footgear used. The emphasis is on readiness for action, which is consistent with the warfare theme, but the key term that is common to Isaiah, Romans and Ephesians is *gospel*, or good news. Once again, therefore, Paul calls his hearers to an outlook that goes beyond the individual soldier's protection to encompass his mission.

Shield of faith is a marvelous and much-quoted image. Unlike some pieces of armor, which are fastened in place to guard only certain parts of the body, a shield can be deployed and maneuvered to fend off all missiles, wherever they are coming from and toward whatever part of the body they are headed. The shield pictured here, unlike the small round shield sometimes used, was large (four feet high by two and one-half feet wide) and shaped like a door. In fact its name, *thyreos*, came from the word for door, *thyra*. Marching side by side holding up these large shields, soldiers could advance on an enemy well protected. Used that way, the shield could be an important part of an offensive thrust, even though it was a defensive piece.

The Old Testament describes God as our shield: "My shield is God Most High, who saves the upright in heart" (Ps 7:10). The faith that saves (Eph 2:8) now becomes an implement of spiritual protection. The shield was often covered with leather and could be presoaked in water to extinguish missiles dipped in tar and set on fire. Without that preparation, a shield made of wood could be set on fire and become a threat to the soldier. We need the shield of faith to *extinguish all the flaming arrows of the evil one*. The devil (v. 11) is now called *the evil one*, as he is in the Lord's Prayer—a reminder of the sinister power against whom we need full protection.

If the *faith* that brings salvation protects us, so does *salvation* itself. Isaiah 59:17, "He put on righteousness as his breastplate, and the helmet of salvation on his head," and 1 Thessalonians 5:8, "But since we belong to the day, let us be self-controlled, putting on faith and love as a breastplate, and the hope of salvation as a helmet," mention both the breastplate (righteousness or love) and the *helmet of salvation*. It is difficult to know just how these relate in the mind of the biblical writers, but one thing is completely clear: the various pieces of armor are interrelated and cannot be analyzed or deployed individually. At the same time there is a subtle shift from the qualities of inherent character implied by the preceding pieces of armor to *salvation* and *the word of God,* which are objective gifts to be received.

Salvation is a basic theme throughout Scripture. The word connotes a range of ways in which God rescues, delivers or redeems those who trust in him. The mind is essential for life and coordination; the head is vulnerable to lethal or incapacitating blows. Thus the soldier needs a *helmet* signifying the saving power of God.

It is often noted that the *sword* is the only offensive piece of equipment listed here. While that is true, its offensive characteristic is that it represents *the word of God,* which has already been implied in verse 15 by *the gospel of peace.* The fact that Paul uses the word for the short rather than the long sword suggests hand-to-hand combat.

Whether or not Paul has in mind the idea of the Messiah slaying the wicked "with the breath of his lips" in Isaiah 11:4 (which immediately precedes the words of v. 5, "Righteousness will be his belt and faithfulness the sash . . ."), the point in this passage is that it is the sword of the *Spirit,* not uniquely that of the Messiah. (Contrast Rev 1:16; 2:12, 16; 19:13-15.) The use of the sword seems to be connected with the preaching of the gospel. That connection appears in the double reference to the Spirit in verses 18-19, which introduces the ministry of prayer, which is then connected with Paul's preaching of the gospel. The connection is further strengthened by the use of the term "ambassador" to describe Paul's gospel ministry.

The Importance of Prayer (6:18-20) Words for prayer, in one form or another, occur four times in verse 18 and once in verse 20. The success of "the gospel of peace" and of the spiritual battle requires prayer, but in truth it is needed *on all occasions.* The Greek word for "all" or "every" also appears four times in verse 18. We should not only pray *on all occasions,* but with *all kinds of prayers and requests,* and there should be prayer with (literally) "all" perseverance for *all the saints.*

The alertness mentioned in verse 18 could allude to the need for being on guard in the spiritual battle just described, as well as to keeping watch in prayer. This is a duty the disciples neglected in Gethsemane: "Then [Jesus] returned to his disciples and found them sleeping. 'Could you men not keep watch with me for one hour?' he asked Peter" (Mt 26:40). First Thessalonians 5:4-11 connects alertness with self-control and spiritual warfare, and 1 Peter 5:8-9 connects it with resistance to Satan.

If Paul knew the importance of praying continually (1 Thess 5:17), how much more can we see accomplished by praying incessantly during all our waking hours! Paul knew people across only a few of the world's time zones; many of us today know, or know of, people for whom we can pray in almost every time zone around the world. Christians in, say, New York can pray Saturday evening for church services, Sunday schools and other special activities concurrently underway on Sunday in Japan. We can receive urgent prayer requests by phone, fax or e-mail and immediately begin intercession.

This powerful call to prayer is not surprising at this point in the letter. Paul has energized his writing of Ephesians with strong elements of prayer. He had barely completed his opening blessing (which itself is a kind of prayer, praising God) when he was motivated to express his prayer for the Ephesians (1:15-23). Then, after passionately explaining the "mystery" entrusted to him, he concluded chapter 3 with another prayer (3:14-21). In chapter 5 one aspect of the Spirit-filled life is thanksgiving.

The question may be asked whether to *pray in the Spirit* is a particular kind of prayer, or ordinary prayer (if there is such a thing) done more

---

6:19 Paul wrote openly of his limitations as a public speaker and seemed to be genuinely modest, even though speakers in his day sometimes postured by professing a lack of eloquence. "When I came to you, brothers, I did not come with eloquence or superior wisdom as I proclaimed to you the testimony about God. . . . My message and

intensely. Also, considering the other references to the Spirit in Ephesians, does this relate to the filling of the Spirit in 5:18? Paul is so conscious of the Holy Spirit that it is hard to conceive of him *not* associating prayer with the Spirit. Just as we could not obey the command to be filled with the Spirit without the active work of the Spirit, so we could not have a full prayer life without reliance on the Spirit. Paul has already written in Romans 8:26-27 that when we do not know what to pray for, it is the Spirit who makes the needed intercession.

When he was addressing a situation where some had become extreme in their use of "tongues," Paul offered his own experience that he did pray in tongues but that when he did so his mind was "unfruitful." Therefore he prayed with his (or "the") spirit, but he also prayed with his (or "the") mind (1 Cor 14:14-15). The context in 1 Corinthians has to do with public meetings and therefore presumably with public rather than private prayer.

In Ephesians he urges prayer *in* (not "with" as seems to be the meaning in 1 Corinthians) the Spirit, and in this case he clearly means the Holy Spirit. It is doubtful whether he is referring to praying in tongues here. More likely he is referring to an abiding spiritual relationship with God, perhaps as described in Jesus' "upper room discourse" (Jn 14—16); both the Holy Spirit and prayer are prominent in that teaching.

The NIV has *with all kinds of prayers and requests,* adding the word *kinds* to *all.* Given the fact that there are various words for prayer in Scripture and that prayer includes confession, worship, petition and intercession, among other expressions, it is appropriate to understand *all* as implying variety. The first noun, *prayers,* is comprehensive, while *requests* is more narrow and referring to petitions. This second word, *deēsis,* recurs before the phrase *for all the saints;* the NIV, however, uses the previous term, *proseuchē* (though in verbal form), since our English phrase "pray for" connotes offering petitions.

In verse 19 Paul asks prayer for himself. He wanted to let every

my preaching were not with wise and persuasive words, but with a demonstration of the Spirit's power, so that your faith might not rest on men's wisdom, but on God's power" (1 Cor 2:1, 4-5).

occasion of speaking be an opportunity not only for witnessing but also for preaching and teaching about *the mystery of the gospel*. This shows again his sense of responsibility to the revelation of the mystery he described in chapter 3.

He was concerned to speak boldly (NIV *fearlessly*) and uses that terminology both in verse 19 and in verse 20. In 2 Timothy 1:7 Paul urged Timothy not to be timid. Here he wants the same deliverance from timidity for himself. This concern was seen in the apostles after they were told not to speak in the name of Jesus. When the apostles prayed, they did not ask for protection, but for boldness, which God gave them through the Holy Spirit (Acts 4:29-31). In Ephesians 6:20, after the words *that I may declare it fearlessly,* Paul adds the brief telltale clause *as I should,* using the Greek word denoting necessity, *dei*. This recalls his earlier determination to preach the gospel without charge and without boasting, "for I am compelled to preach. Woe to me if I do not preach the gospel!" (1 Cor 9:16).

By praying for Paul, the Ephesian Christians could participate with him in that obligation, together asking their great God to give his servant evangelism and missions, even to the point of boldness as *an ambassador in chains*. The role of an ambassador in modern international relations is to represent her or his government. So it was when the Roman emperor was represented by the person he designated. The same was true of an apostle, who represented the Lord. Normally an ambassador has diplomatic immunity, and an embassy is a place of refuge. In Paul's case he is exposed to the indignity of *chains*.

One naturally thinks of the great apostle as always ready to speak well. Paul was, however, very conscious of his need of the Spirit's help (1 Cor 2:1, 4-5). He was also concerned to speak boldly, without fear (Eph 6:19-20). By praying for Paul, other Christians could participate with him in evangelism and missions. The same principle is true today.

6:20 Some years ago Markus Barth drew a graphic contrast between secular ambassadors and Paul, the *ambassador in chains*. Commentators since then have been struck by that image, and it is worth citing here. After noting that in Paul's day decorative gold chains were sometimes worn by people of social stature, Barth says, "On festive occasions ambassadors wear such chains in order to reveal the riches, power and dignity

□ Concluding Encouragement (6:21-24)

This letter includes fewer personal greetings than others Paul wrote. In fact, there is no named recipient of the greetings, just the implication in the benediction, *Peace to the brothers* (v. 23), that Paul wishes to send his regards to whoever may read or hear what he has written. This is not surprising, considering that its contents are general, apparently intended for more than one church to read.

A letter had to be carried by someone, however, and so a personal touch, a reference to Tychicus, appears in the conclusion. But Tychicus does more than carry mail; he brings to the recipients personal news about Paul. Even this was not merely to convey information but specifically *for this very purpose*, to bring encouragement.

The paragraph about Tychicus is virtually identical to the one in Colossians 4:7-8. It could be seen as demonstrating the connection between Ephesians and Colossians, though some see it as a device used by a writer other than Paul who wrote Ephesians as an expression of Pauline thought. If this were the case, it would be an artless reproduction of the Colossians passage, somewhat as students sometimes only slightly modify passages they copy from a source (see the introduction).

The New Testament includes three other references to Tychicus besides those here and in Colossians. He appears with Paul on part of Paul's third missionary journey (Acts 20:4). He and Trophimus were from the province of Asia. They went to Troas and may well have been with Paul at other times; we do not know. From 2 Timothy 4:12 we gather that Tychicus was with Paul during his imprisonment at that time, and was sent to Ephesus. This of course provides another link with those to whom he is to carry the present letter, assuming that Ephesus was at least one of its destinations. Titus 3:12 says that Paul intends to send Tychicus to Crete, apparently to relieve Titus so he could leave that post and visit Paul. The picture we get from all this, including the description of him here in Ephesians, is warm and appreciative of him and his service

---

of the government they represent. Because Paul serves Christ crucified, he considers the painful iron prison chains as most appropriate insignia for the representation of his Lord" (Barth 1974b:782).

6:21-22 The reference to Tychicus is an integral part of discussions on the authorship of Ephesians. Such matters are taken up in the introduction.

to the Lord. He is trusted to be a courier, but there were other ways to send mail through the Roman post. Paul wanted Tychicus to have a personal ministry of encouragement, part of which would be to bring a firsthand report about Paul.

The letter concludes, in typical ancient fashion, with a benediction on the recipients. Paul desires them to have *peace,* and *love with faith.* These are words familiar from the Pauline letters. Love and faith were linked in 1:15 and 3:17, and faith is an important element in God's gift of salvation (2:8-10). *Grace* is also of special importance in Ephesians 2 and elsewhere. Paul frequently ends (as well as begins) his letters with a reference to the grace of the Lord, but given the theological and personal importance of grace in the body of his letter, it is especially significant here.

The concluding words present one final exegetical issue. The last two words are, in the Greek, a prepositional phrase: literally, "in immortality." Their position makes them important; they will remain in the minds of the readers and hearers. But do they refer back to the verbal idea in the participle, "loving . . . in a way that is deathless and imperishable"? That is the understanding of the NIV, *with an undying love.* Do they instead refer to the unexpressed verb in the benediction, "be," so that it means "May grace be with all in a way that is without mortal corruption"? A prepositional phrase basically can refer to the verbal idea or to a noun or noun phrase. These first two possibilities see the phrase as a verbal modifier. But it could also modify a noun or noun phrase. Its closest proximity is to the words *Lord Jesus Christ,* but the phrasing Christ-in-immortality, while grammatically possible and theologically sound, is awkward. Nevertheless, it is an attractive possibility (see Snodgrass 1996:364-65).

Another strong possibility is that it refers back to the word *grace.* This is supported by Andrew Lincoln (1990:466-68) and Rudolf Schnackenburg (1991:291), among others. The position of F. F. Bruce (1984:415-16) is not strongly expressed, but there is justification in his opinion for linking the phrase with *grace* in a comitative sense, the attachment of words in a sequence. This is attractive because of the importance of grace in the letter. While it could be considered unlikely because of the distance between *grace,* which opens the sentence, and the modifying phrase, which closes it, it is not impossible. Paul's meaning could be "Grace be with all . . . the grace that is indestructible." If Paul had wanted the phrase to modify *grace* and also wanted to have "in immortality" as the concluding climactic words, he would have little choice other than to put *grace* first and allow the awkwardness of the resultant sentence structure to stand.

J. Armitage Robinson (1904:217-20) did an extensive historical study of the word and proposed an elegant rendering, "in that endless and unbroken life in which love has triumphed over death and dissolution." The fact that there are such rich possible interpretations is a testimony to the breadth of the thought and theology of the author of Ephesians, but infinitely more to the extraordinary grace of God portrayed in this epistle.

Bibliography

Abbott, T. K.
1897   *Epistles to the Ephesians and to the Colossians*. The
            International Critical Commentary. Edinburgh: T & T Clark.
Arnold, Clinton E.
1989   *Ephesians: Power and Magic*. New York: Cambridge
            University Press.

1992   *Powers of Darkness*. Downers Grove, Ill.: InterVarsity Press.

Aune, David E.
1988   *Greco-Roman Literature and the New Testament: Selected
            Forms and Genres*. Atlanta: Scholars Press.
Banks, Robert
1988   *Paul's Idea of Community: The Early House Churches in
            Their Historical Setting*. Grand Rapids, Mich.: Eerdmans.
Bartchy, S. Scott
1973   ΜΑΛΛΟΝ ΧΡΗΣΑΙ: *First Century Slavery and the Interpre-
            tation of 1 Corinthians 7:21*. Missoula, Mont.: Scholars Press.
Barth, Markus
1974a   *Ephesians 1-3*. Anchor Bible 34. Garden City, N.Y.:
            Doubleday.

1974b   *Ephesians 4-6*. Anchor Bible 34a. Garden City, N.Y.:
            Doubleday.
Bauer, Walter
1979   *A Greek-English Lexicon of the New Testament and Other
            Early Christian Literature*. Edited and translated by
            William F. Arndt, F. Wilbur Gingrich and Frederick W.
            Danker. 2nd ed. Chicago: University of Chicago Press.

Behm, J.
1964   "ἀρραβών." In *Theological Dictionary of the New Testament*, 1:475. Edited by Gerhard Kittel. 10 vols. Grand Rapids, Mich.: Eerdmans.

Best, Ernest
1993   "Ministry in Ephesians." Irish Biblical Studies 5:146-466.

Bratcher, Robert G., and Eugene A. Nida
1982   *A Handbook on Paul's Letter to the Ephesians*. New York: United Bible Societies.

Brown, Colin
1976   "Head." In *The New International Dictionary of New Testament Theology*, 2:156-63. Edited by Colin Brown. 3 vols. Grand Rapids, Mich.: Zondervan.

Bruce, F. F.
1984   *The Epistles to the Colossians, to Philemon and to the Ephesians*. New International Commentary on the New Testament. Grand Rapids, Mich.: Eerdmans.

Calvin, John
1948   *Commentaries on the Epistles of Paul to the Galatians and Ephesians*. Original 1584. Translated by Rev. W. Pringle. Grand Rapids, Mich.: Eerdmans.

Caragounis, Chrys C.
1977   *The Ephesian Mysterion*. Coniectanea Biblica. Lund, Sweden: CWK Gleerup.

Danker, F. W.
1982   "Ephesians, Epistle to." In *The International Standard Bible Encyclopedia*, 2:109-14. Edited by Geoffrey W. Bromiley. 4 vols. Grand Rapids, Mich.: Eerdmans.

Dunn, J. D. G.
1970   *Baptism in the Holy Spirit*. London: SCM Press, 1970.

Eichler, J.
1976   "Inheritance, Lot, Portion." In *The New International Dictionary of New Testament Theology*, 2:295-303. Edited by Colin Brown. 3 vols. Grand Rapids, Mich.: Zondervan.

Esser, H.-H.
1976   "Grace, Spiritual Gifts." In *The New International Dictionary of New Testament Theology*, 2:115-24. Edited by Colin Brown. 3 vols. Grand Rapids, Mich.: Zondervan.

Fee, Gordon
   1987   *The First Epistle to the Corinthians.* New International Commentary on the New Testament. Grand Rapids, Mich.: Eerdmans.

Fung, Ronald Y. K.
   1980   "Charismatic Versus Organized Ministry? An Examination of an Alleged Synthesis." *Evangelical Quarterly* 52:195-214.

   1982   "The Nature of the Ministry According to Paul." *Evangelical Quarterly* 54:29-146.

Giles, Kevin
   1989   *Patterns of Ministry Among the First Christians.* Victoria, Australia: Collins Dove.

Gordon, V. R.
   1988   "Saints." In *The International Standard Bible Encyclopedia,* 4:282-83. Edited by Geoffrey W. Bromiley. 4 vols. Grand Rapids, Mich.: Eerdmans.

Grudem, Wayne A.
   1985   "Does *Kephalē* Mean 'Source' or 'Authority Over' in Greek Literature? A Survey of 2,336 Examples." *Trinity Journal* n.s. 6:38-59.

   1991   "Appendix 1: The Meaning of *Kephalē* ('Head'): A Response to Recent Studies." In *Recovering Biblical Manhood and Womanhood: A Response to Evangelical Feminism.* Edited by John Piper and Wayne Grudem. Wheaton, Ill.: Crossway.

Günther, W., and
W. Bauder
   1978   "Sin." In *The New International Dictionary of New Testament Theology,* 3:573-87. Edited by Colin Brown. 3 vols. Grand Rapids, Mich.: Zondervan.

Guthrie, Donald
   1981   *New Testament Theology.* Downers Grove, Ill.: InterVarsity Press.

Harris, Murray J.
   1992   *Jesus as God: The New Testament Use of Theos in Reference to Jesus.* Grand Rapids, Mich.: Baker Book House.

Holmberg, Bengt
   1980   *Paul and Power.* Philadelphia: Fortress.

Kroeger,
Catherine C.
   1987   "The Classical Concept of Head as 'Source.'" Appendix 3

in Gretchen Gaebelein Hull, *Equal to Serve*, pp. 267-83. Old Tappan, N.J.: Revell.

1993   "Head." In *Dictionary of Paul and His Letters*, pp. 375-77. Edited by Gerald F. Hawthorne, Ralph P. Martin and Daniel G. Reid. Downers Grove, Ill.: InterVarsity Press.

Ladd, George Eldon

1974   *A Theology of the New Testament*. Grand Rapids, Mich.: Eerdmans.

Liddell, Henry G.,
Robert Scott and
Henry Stuart
Jones

1968   *A Greek-English Lexicon*. Oxford: Clarendon.

Liefeld, Walter L.

1986   "Prayer." In *The International Standard Bible Encyclopedia*, 3:931-39. Edited by G. W. Bromiley. 4 vols. Grand Rapids, Mich.: Eerdmans.

1988   "Salvation." In *The International Standard Bible Encyclopedia*, 4:287-95. Edited by Geoffrey W. Bromiley. Grand Rapids, Mich.: Eerdmans.

Lincoln, Andrew T.

1990   *Ephesians*. Word Biblical Commentary 42. Dallas: Word.

Mickelsen, Alvera, ed.

1986   *Women, Authority and the Bible*. Downers Grove, Ill.: InterVarsity Press.

Moo, Douglas J.

1996   *The Epistle to the Romans*. New International Commentary on the New Testament. Grand Rapids, Mich.: Eerdmans.

Morris, Leon

1994   *Expository Reflections on the Letter to the Ephesians*. Grand Rapids, Mich.: Baker Book House, 1994.

Moule, C. F. D.

1959   *An Idiom Book of New Testament Greek*. 2nd ed. Cambridge: Cambridge University Press.

O'Brien, Peter T.

1977   *Introductory Thanksgiving in the Letters of Paul*. Supplements to *Novum Testamentum* 49. Leiden: E. J. Brill.

Oepke, Albrecht,
and Karl Georg
Kuhn
1967   "ὅπλον κτλ." In *Theological Dictionary of the New Testament*, 5:292-315. Edited by Gerhard Friedrich. 10 vols. Grand Rapids, Mich.: Eerdmans.

Peterson, Eugene
1993   *The Message: The New Testament in Contemporary English.* Colorado Springs, Colo.: NavPress.

Porter, Stanley
1989   *Verbal Aspect in the Greek of the New Testament, with Reference to Tense and Mood.* Studies in Biblical Greek 1. Edited by Donald A. Carson. New York: Peter Lang.

1992a   *Idioms of the Greek New Testament.* Biblical Languages: Greek 2. Sheffield, U.K.: JSOT Press.

1992b   "Principalities and Powers: Opponents of the Church." *Evangelical Review of Theology* 16:353-84.

1993   *Biblical Greek Language and Linguistics: Open Questions in Current Research.* Supplement Series 80. Edited by S. Porter and D. A. Carson. Sheffield, U.K.: JSOT Press.

Roberts, J. H.
1993   "The Enigma of Ephesians." *Neotestamentica* 27:93-106.

Robinson, J.
Armitage
1904   *St. Paul's Epistle to the Ephesians.* 2nd ed. London: James Clarke.

Sampley, J. Paul
1971   *And the Two Shall Become One Flesh.* Society for New Testament Studies Monograph Series 16, 9-51. Cambridge: Cambridge University Press.

Schlier, Heinrich
1965   "κεφαλή, ἀνακεφαλαιόομαι." In *Theological Dictionary of the New Testament,* 3:673-82. Edited by Gerhard Kittel. 10 vols. Grand Rapids, Mich.: Eerdmans.

Schnackenburg,
Rudolf
1991   *The Epistle to the Ephesians.* Edinburgh: T & T Clark.

Schwartzbeck, R.
1991   "Divine Warrior Typology in Ephesians 6:10-20: A

Neglected Element in the Study of Spiritual Warfare." Ph.D. dissertation, Trinity Evangelical Divinity School.

Smith, Gary V.
1975   "Paul's Use of Psalm 68:18 in Ephesians 4:8." *Journal of the Evangelical Theological Society* 18:181-89.

Snodgrass, Klyne
1996   *Ephesians*. The NIV Application Commentary. Grand Rapids, Mich.: Zondervan.

Stott, John R. W.
1979   *The Message of Ephesians*. Originally published as *God's New Society*. Downers Grove, Ill.: InterVarsity Press.

Strickland, W.
1993   *The Law, the Gospel and the Modern Christian*. Grand Rapids, Mich.: Zondervan.

Swartley, Willard
1983   *Slavery, Sabbath, War and Women*. Scottdale, Penn.: Herald.

Thielmann, Frank
1995   *Paul and the Law: A Contextual Approach*. Downers Grove, Ill.: InterVarsity Press.

Westermann, W. L.
1964   *The Slave Systems of Greek and Roman Antiquity*. 3rd ed. Philadelphia: American Philosophical Society.

White, L. M.
1987   "Social Authority in the House Church Setting and Ephesians 4:1-16." *Restoration Quarterly* 29:209-28.